No

The Lee Bullen Story

Lee Bullen with Alan Biggs

No Bull

The Lee Bullen Story

Lee Bullen with Alan Biggs

Vertical Editions
www.verticaleditions.com

First published in the United Kingdom in 2013 by Vertical Editions Ltd. Paperback edition published in 2014

Vertical Editions Ltd, Unit 4a, Snaygill Industrial Estate, Skipton, North Yorkshire BD23 2QR
www.verticaleditions.com

ISBN 978-1-904091-81-3

A CIP catalogue record for this book is available from the British Library

Cover design by HBA, York

Printed and bound by CMP (uk) Limited

My love and gratitude to all those closest to me, to all those who've shared my life starting with my mum and dad, Margaret and John, who gave me and my brothers such a great upbringing. Also, of course, to Kerry and to Nicola and to my great kids, Jay and Jodie. Hope there's nothing here to embarrass you!

Contents

Acknowledgements

It's my life laid bare, warts and all, but it's only after completing a project on this scale that you realise how little you could have accomplished on your own. A schoolteacher pal in Sheffield, Steve Johnson, was the first to hear that I wished to make some ordered sense of my tumbledown career. I'm grateful to Steve for laying down some of the groundwork in the early stages.

That's where it stayed until I was approached out of the blue by a certain friendly neighbourhood journalist. Alan Biggs suggested there was a good book in me – so he's really the one to blame! My thanks to Alan and to Karl Waddicor at Vertical Editions (with whom he'd a couple of previous books published) for giving me this opportunity.

Alan and myself would also like to thank a Sheffield footballing legend, David Ford, for providing his gastro pub, The Cross Scythes at Totley in Sheffield, as our 'office' for the duration of our labours. And thanks to pub manager Stuart for finding quiet corners of this busy establishment. It was courtesy of Alan's tight expense account that the beverages never got stronger than coffee – and perhaps just as well!

Last but by no means least, I'd like to thank all the managers I've worked for and in particular Chris Turner, who not only brought me to the club where I enjoyed the biggest day of my football life but who also kindly agreed to provide a generous contribution to this book.

Prologue

Lee Bullen is a man of the world. The real world. Not the world of flash motors and country mansions. He's had real jobs, knowing what it's like to work nine-to-five and beyond for a pittance of pay. But this is also a bloke who, in a career as a journeyman footballer, has lived the stuff of dreams.

As such, Bullen is a man of the world in the proper sense. He's chased the rainbow across the globe and back from his early days with Dunfermline to his crowning glory as the Sheffield Wednesday skipper who lifted a trophy in front of nearly 60,000 fans at the Millennium Stadium. In between times, he played in Australia, Hong Kong, Greece and Scotland.

Along the way, he achieved the Roy of the Rovers feat of playing in every position on the field – in the course of a single season. Even as a striker-turned-defender, Lee could never envisage standing between the sticks, but, like a lot of things in his life, it just happened. Oh, but only with the help of relentless hard work along the way.

He's juggled jobs, toiling six and seven days a week to make it happen. In Scotland he worked full-time and played part-time. Latterly it's come full-circle for Bully, combining coaching back at Sheffield Wednesday with being a partner in his girlfriend's estate agency. Even then, he took an unusual route, having been assistant manager of Falkirk in the Scottish Premier League just before going into business.

This is the story of a steely Scot making his own way in the world. And around it. Above all, Lee Bullen has a sense of perspective on life that makes his journey – and the tales along the way – a refreshing antidote to all football's excesses as well as being a thoroughly entertaining ride. Here's your chance to share it.

Alan Biggs

1

You Can Even Eat the Dishes ...

It's my Friday morning fix. Radio on full blast, driving to work listening to Chris Evans. Waiting, just waiting for that special time of the week. And here we go, sing along now ...

'Who can take a sunrise (who can take a sunrise) – sprinkle it with dew ...'

I'm singing with the best of them, even with the car windows down if it's a sunny day. Do love that Candyman song of Sammy Davis Junior. Makes you feel good and makes me glad of the life I lead ... including a couple of lines that sum up a lot of things for me ...

'Now you can talk about your childhood wishes – you can even eat the dishes.'

And so I can. Talk I mean! Here's a little about how the childhood wishes came true for me before the real story begins. Hold on to your hats. It takes me to the far side of the world and back ... back to the Millennium Stadium in Cardiff on a Sammy Davis type sunny day in 2005.

Unbelievable view from the coach here in Cardiff. Never seen anything like it in my life. Blue and white everywhere. At Sheffield Wednesday we share the same colours as our play-off final opponents Hartlepool. But there's more than 40,000 of our fans down here and as we turn a corner near the ground, Wednesdayites are packing the street with their balloons and banners. One guy's running with a full pint of beer to catch up with our coach. He keeps spilling some. By the time he reaches us he's got an empty pot. Let's hope this is a glass half-full sort of day for us ...

It is! The dressing room afterwards is awash with champagne. Everyone's hugging and dancing. I slump against a wall, drinking from a can of beer. I'm mentally and physically drained but it's the biggest buzz I've ever had.

'Cover it with chocolate and a miracle or two. Oh, the Candyman can ...'

Back in the real world now and more of that fantasy stuff later. But dreams can and do come true. Miracles do happen if you work for them. Mine happened because of a tearful decision I made – and somehow carried out – to leave my family in Scotland and fly out alone to Australia. My football career was going nowhere. If I hadn't got on that plane, if I hadn't left my family crying back at home, then I wouldn't be doing this book. But that's a story for later.

It all begins in the front room of a small house near Edinburgh. Well, actually it's a lounge and dining room combined. That is my first football 'pitch.' It's there from the age of about four that I play my first competitive games. There are 'goals' at either end. One is a settee and the other is a back door. The opposition is my younger brother Gary.

2

It's Pronounced Pennycook!

Whenever anybody other than a fellow Scot asks me where I'm from, I usually say Edinburgh. It's simpler. It's also close enough to the truth. And it has the advantage of avoiding being met with a blank expression. Everybody's heard of the kind of house we lived in. It was a Wimpey home. But when anyone is presented with the name 'Penicuik' you can see the eyes glaze over. Wish I had a pound for every different pronunciation I've heard and I suppose that's part of the charm of the place. But just for the record, before we get properly started, the correct phonetic version is 'Pennycook.' It's a little town with a population of 16,000 and literally means 'Hill of the Cuckoo.' Now why that is, I couldn't tell you. But I suppose it could explain some of what's happened to me since!

Actually my childhood could not have been more ordinary. And I mean that in the best possible way. It was a nice, settled upbringing. There we were living in a Wimpey house on a new estate. Small but cosy might be a way to describe it. 'We' were my dad John, my mum Margaret (both still going strong, I'm glad to say) and my two younger brothers, Gary and Glyn. Now Glyn didn't make his entrance until I was seven, which is perhaps just as well for him! It was with Gary, two years my junior, that

I enjoyed my first 'competitive' football.

The lounge and dining room were connected and ran the width of the house. My first set of goals were the back door at one end and the settee at the other. They were only about five yards apart but that was plenty in our own little world. I suppose I was just about three or four, and Gary only a toddler when we played our first game. From that point on, things just got rougher and louder. It was only a light plastic ball that we used but it would bounce off the walls and the table, knocking things on the floor. As we got older, the fights would start. And on at least several occasions, the ball somehow made its way onto the heads and into the faces of both our parents.

Mum was very house-proud and yet you'll be surprised to hear she just let us get on with it. As for Dad, he would join in with the games! So I suppose Mum had no chance and just took the least line of resistance. She tended to stay at home, giving her plenty of time to straighten it up, while Dad went to work for a crystal glass factory. In fact, he was employed there all his working life. Just as well nothing of what was made there found its way into our living room.

Dad was my inspiration when it came to football. He played for the RAF during his national service and went on to non-league level in Scotland. Once he turned out in a game at Norwich City's Carrow Road. A knee injury stopped him playing but he stayed involved by coaching at a local boys club. I became one of his signings. Well, not just his ... there was another coach down there by the name of Alex Young.

This was none other than the 'Golden Vision' of Everton fame, a Scot who had come home after a great career in England. After starting at Hearts and moving south, he scored 87 goals in 273 games for Everton between 1960 and

1968. He won an FA Cup winners medal in '66 in a game that older Sheffield Wednesday fans will not need reminding about. It finished 3-2 against the Owls. Anyway, Alex Young had a son in the same boys club team so he would lend a hand preparing the lads. My Dad could only pinch himself about that. This was a man who was rightfully installed as a Goodison legend. He also won the league title during his eight years there. After that, Alex – or Alec as we called him – moved back to Scotland to run his family's upholstery business in Edinburgh. He had started out with Hearts, the team I supported as a kid. Brother Gary was a rebel – he followed Hibs. So you can imagine the arguments.

We were lucky in having a decent patch of grass at the back of our house where we used to have inter-street games with neighbouring kids. At school I played for Combank Primary and later for Penicuik High School. But a lot of my grounding came from my Dad and the Esk Mills Boys Club team. I was a striker and always pretty quick. In fact, I relied on my pace – which might surprise supporters of some of the teams I've played for! I suppose it helped that I was only of average height – it was only when I was 15 that I started to shoot up to be the ugly beast you see before you now! And it was then that I joined Hutchison Vale Boys Club, which was very well known and respected in Scotland, en route to signing for Dunfermline Athletic as a youth player.

Already, I had heroes. We all do, don't we? The great Kenny Dalglish was a top player in Scotland and I admired him. Then along came the first World Cup I remember. It was Argentina 1978 and the host nation won it, courtesy of great players such as Mario Kempes. But my favourite memory is of the brilliant goal Archie Gemmill scored for Scotland against Holland. The rest is best forgotten as 'Ally's Army' – led by Ally McLeod – beat a hasty retreat from the tournament. My real idols were closer to home. Watching Hearts, my favourite was little John Robertson, a legendary goalscorer for the club around that time. Later John became a manager in Scotland and he's still around the game now. In fact, I speak to him quite a lot in my current role which is strange considering he was such a hero of mine as a kid.

Looking back, I'm grateful to my parents that football wasn't my only option. Armed with nine 'O' levels, or GCSEs as they are called nowadays, I went to night school. But I didn't stick at it and went to work at 16 for the Alliance and Leicester Building Society. Sounds grand but I was just an office boy really, making coffee and filing stuff. And the reason I went there was to start making money, simple as that. It was around that time in 1988 that I signed schoolboy forms at Dunfermline who were in the top league. I was playing for the boys club as well besides working. A busy boy!

I think Mum was a bit disappointed I didn't go to college or university. Both she and Dad – who would come to watch all my matches – were very supportive. As a by the way, I was also into golf and badminton as a kid – and I won the high jump at primary school. I had my fair share of scrapes for a young lad, too, though I was never in any serious trouble. There would be some small-town local rivalry between Penicuik and a place up the road called Loanhead. Only five miles separated the two and, in between there were smaller places called Bilston and Roslin. If there was a disco in Roslin, it was typical for a bit of bother to break out between lads from the rival towns either side. I do remember being chased through some fields one dark night and ending up waist deep in a bog!

Another nasty memory from my youth is of getting a little too close to the action at Tynecastle. At Penicuik the coach was a guy called John Frame who also ran the junior supporters club at Hearts. There was this occasion when John arranged for me and a few of the others from the team to work as ball boys there. It was a one-off opportunity as a Scottish Cup semi-final was being staged at the ground. I have to say it was absolutely horrible. There we were in Hearts tracksuits getting roundly abused by fans of two rival clubs. I remember being spat on and all sorts. An awful experience that I would not wish to repeat but character-forming, shall we say.

Anyway, some of my mates had gone to Hearts or Hibs, lucky so-and-sos that they were. I never got the opportunity, so Dunfermline was my best bet. And they went on to release me. Doesn't sound too promising so far, does it? So I signed non-league with Penicuik. That meant training two nights a week while working Monday to Friday for Alliance and Leicester. I'd get £12 a week from the football club and £5,400 a year from the day job. Funny how you never forget the exact amounts you were paid in your first employment. It was hard graft but it formed a work ethic in me that has stayed to this day. And, when I finally got my break as a full-timer in football, I appreciated it ten times more than I would have done in other circumstances.

In winter I'd never see daylight. I had to be up at six for a bus to work and would arrive home in the dusk. But that never held any fears for me and it doesn't to this day. As I speak, I'm working five mornings a week for Sheffield Wednesday at Hillsborough and five afternoons at Spencers estate agency in Sheffield, plus evenings as well. But then it has to be said that Nicola, my girlfriend – who is now in charge of the family firm – works twice as hard as I do. It's not until they step out of the football bubble that many players realise what the real world is like.

In particular, there's a massive difference between playing and coaching. You'd arrive for training as a player and everything would be done for you, right down to the cones being put out. As a coach, you are preparing the training and analysing the opposition. Then there's coping with the demands of the modern media, like your young players saying the wrong things on Twitter. You have to educate them, tackling stuff outside the game that still has an effect on it.

I digress. You've got me rambling here. But then that was also the state of my career at that time, and I've done plenty of rambling since. I left Penicuik when Meadowbank Thistle – later reformed as Livingston – spotted the young striker who was now a six-footer. This was second-tier football in Scotland and I was 19. Nothing much else had changed, it was still part-time. But I got my first break in league football and I was buzzing before my debut against Montrose. I even set up our goal in a 1-1 draw. But from then on I was in and out of the team.

This can be normal for a young player, although in my case I was very much hampered by the fact that if I did anything wrong I took it to heart. If anyone had a go at me on the field I'd be 'lost' for the next ten minutes. As you get older, you learn to play the moment and not be affected by normal things like this. I got pretty down and felt my only chance had gone in relation to earning a full-time career.

After a year at Meadowbank Thistle I moved to Stenhousemuir in 1990. Believe it or not, I became their record signing at about £6,000. However impressive that might sound, I dropped a league to make the move, and I was still part-time and no better off financially. Actually, I was worse off. From £35 a week at Meadowbank, I went down to £25 at Stenhousemuir. I made the sacrifice simply because I felt I had a better chance of playing and the manager of the club made me feel welcome.

But the season that followed was a story of constant knock-backs. I had to question whether I'd ever make it. I was 20 by then and pretty disillusioned, desperately needing a boost to my enthusiasm and confidence. The kick I needed came in the shape of yet another move, this time to Whitburn Juniors and a twist of fate that led me to try my luck on the other side of the planet.

3

Down and Out – then Down Under

My first pick-me-up was joining Whitburn Juniors. The second was flying out to Australia. As you do! It was 12,000 miles away from home that my career began to take off – and yet the two courses of action described above were very closely linked, as I'll explain. Before I did anything I had to recover my love for football. That's where Whitburn came in, along with a fantastic manager called Derek Strickland who provided a wonderful boost to my confidence.

I left Stenhousemuir halfway through my two-year contract simply because I was drifting out of the picture. After going back into non-league at Whitburn I scored goals for fun. I was top scorer in 1991-92 and 1992-93 with 24 and 22 goals respectively. This was at a town of some 12,000 people in West Lothian, a similar size to Penicuik and a place where I felt at home. You'd never guess the small-town boy was about to pack his bags for Australia now would you? I was being tipped for a call-up to Scotland's non-league team and life was fun again. Well, at least the football side of it.

The fact was that however much the football compensated, I was feeling downright miserable in my day job. And when you consider that I still wasn't going anywhere when it came to a full-time football career, something had to give further down the line. At Alliance and Leicester I had worked my way up from Arrears to the Repossessions Department.

Let me tell you, this was a very dubious reward in terms of promotion. It was a time of 15% interest rates. Some very genuine people were failing to hold on to their homes. It was distressing to see the hardship they faced and continued to suffer. Of course, there were always those who played the system but there were many others struggling to keep up with their mortgage payments for very sincere reasons. There would be an unexpected pregnancy or a sudden job loss. Many good people were hurt for no fault of their own and in my role at work there was absolutely nothing I could do for them. It was hard to swallow. My salary was decent, I suppose. It had climbed to around £15,000 a year. But the job was no longer for me. Taking into account my football ambitions, there was only one thing for it. Head to the other side of the world! Bit drastic, but there you go. Pretty obvious when you think about it ...

Not that the idea had ever occurred to me, of course. It came through a friendship with a lad called Billy McPhee whose father (also Billy) had played for Dundee United. Billy was at a similar crossroads to me. His dad had played with a guy called Joe Watson who had emigrated to become a football manager in Australia. Billy just said: 'Do you fancy going over for a year?'

He reckoned there was nothing to lose. We could just take our chances there and if it didn't work out we could always come back. In the meantime, Joe Watson said he couldn't guarantee us anything at his club in New South Wales but that he had plenty of contacts in the game out there. Joe had lived in Australia so long he had got full citizenship. He even played for Australia against Scotland in a World Cup qualifier at Hampden in 1985 where goals from Davie

Cooper and Frank McAvennie saw us through. 'Us' being the Scots, of course.

The proposal was to go out on a travel-work visa. Seemed like a plan. You had to have £3,000 in the bank to fly out there and we got our savings together. It's the sort of venture I would never have contemplated on my own. The fact that I was going with a pal was all-important to me. Then, a month before we were due to depart, Billy phoned to say he would have to pull out. I was devastated but the circumstances were much more harrowing for him. His mum and dad had been separated for a while at that point and suddenly the money wasn't there for his trip. Billy's mum had run into financial difficulties with her business and the money his dad had put aside for the trip was now being used to bail out his mum. I was lucky enough to have sold my car which gave me the cash I needed.

But what should I do now? It was a massive dilemma. Eventually I thought I just had to go for it. I didn't want to get to 40 and wonder what would have happened if I'd plucked up the courage. What also persuaded me was that my mum had a brother and a sister living out in Australia. That was my safety net. But the doubts nagged away at me right up to the moment I stepped on the plane. One voice was telling me to go and the other was telling me to stay.

Even now my eyes fill up when I remember the scene at Edinburgh airport for the first leg of my journey flying to London. My family were all there to wave me off. My mum was crying and my dad was fighting back the tears as well. So was I. Big time. I was leaving behind a girlfriend besides my family. In London, where I spent some time before the next leg of my journey, the doubts crept back. I wasn't so far away that I couldn't change my mind. Had I wavered I wouldn't be writing this book. Wouldn't have got married and had kids, so many things.

It's probably typical of the way my life has worked out that I flew round the world the opposite way. That is, I flew west instead of east. It's the way I'd arranged things with Billy and one of the stopovers was in Hawaii. It's a great place to see but not quite the same when you are stuck on your own. Again, it was a time for being alone with your thoughts. One night I dragged myself out for a walk and went into a nightclub. There was this Bermudian guy I met who was the night porter at the hotel. He was great – every lonely traveller needs to meet somebody like him. From the off he looked after me. He took me around and even had me playing in organised games of football.

And so on to Sydney – via Raratonga and Auckland, New Zealand (remember, we were flying round the other way round.) Finally, there was no turning back. I resolved that I would give it three months and see what happened. Uncle Alistair picked me up at the airport. He lived on the outskirts of the city, which was about a 45 minute drive from the club Joe Watson managed. This was called Stanmore CYC. The CYC stands for Cypriot Youth Club.

There are lots of ethnic-based teams in Australia. Stanmore played in the top division of the New South Wales State League – one level below the National League. It was a British style of football – very physical and hard-working and I'd put it at about Conference standard. Crowds would be between 1,000 and 3,000. I was part-time again (the story of my life to this point) but the money was okay and they fixed me up with a job to go with it. In fact, I had two part-time jobs while playing in Australia. One was with a removals company and the other with an electronics firm. I really loved that second one because I ended up driving forklift trucks around a warehouse. Great fun!

As for the football, that was a serious business. No matter where you are, when you join a new club the first thing you have to conquer is the changing room. A football dressing room is the most cavemanish place on the entire planet. It can be horrendous for a new guy coming in. The be-all and end-all for me is that you are up against it until you can win over your own team-mates, never mind the fans. Outside the club, there was another Scottish bloke over there called Stuart Porter. You see, it's true what they say – we do turn up everywhere! Instantly, we developed a close friendship. Stuart was the one who got me that forklift truck work. He was a warehouse supervisor for a massive company called Honeywell.

Things went okay on the field, which was still the main point of the exercise, and after a couple of months living with my uncle I got my own apartment in an area called Cronulla. All the same, there was a lot of hoo-ha about the type of visa I had. It was a travel visa which meant I was only allowed to stay with one employer for three months. In the event, I was offered a contract to the end of the season with Stanmore and was glad to accept. But it was still a culture shock in that dressing room.

For starters, I was only 21 and the majority of the players were in their mid-to-late 30s. But the even bigger difference was the language. Because it was a Greek-Cypriot team most of the players would talk to each other in Greek. That's natural enough, I suppose. But the way they spoke was very intimidating. I couldn't believe it when they would rant and rave, calling each other 'wogs' and all sorts. Later on, I would play in Greece and I can now understand some of what went on from that experience. But at the time I was thinking: 'What the hell's going on here?'

As time went on I came to realise they were a fantastic

bunch and they began to see that I could play a bit. I think they also appreciated that I tried to get involved despite the language barrier. We'd go out after a game and I'd be there with them. Probably I wouldn't say a word all night – but I'd still be there drinking in their company. I spent the majority of the season with Stanmore, scoring about seven goals in a dozen games. It was all new to me and as no-one knew me I could just go out and be myself. At home it could be very difficult to recover from one bad season because everyone knows everyone in Scotland.

4

Wollongong to Hong Kong ...

Wollongong was just a 40-minute drive to the south of Sydney. It was a lot, lot further away in terms of status. At the time Wollongong Wolves (now South Coast Wolves FC) played in the Australian National League whereas Stanmore were a regional outfit. There was an overlap in the two fixture programmes so a few of the Stanmore lads would play for Wollongong as well. That was a bit bizarre to say the least, although there was a logical explanation. The National League contracts would run for only nine months so players were allowed to link up with state sides in the close-season. And state teams were only too happy to let their best players moonlight in the big league so that they could attract some big names by return.

Anyway, Wollongong had a British coach called David Ratcliffe and he invited me down there for a chat after Joe Watson had spoken to him on my behalf. I ended up training with them for three months but didn't get to play because of problems with my visa. That was frustrating. I'd been promised about £400 a week and I was doing well in training but I couldn't play because of the type of visa I had. It was only when I had a sudden approach about possibly playing in Hong Kong that the red tape magically started to untangle. Wollongong said they had sorted out the visa but still nothing happened on that front. There was just a wall of silence. I don't know whether the fault was with the manager or the board, but it was disappointing because I knew I was making a good impression in training.

The Hong Kong connection came via a phone call out of the blue from an agent called Tom Sermanni. Tom, who incidentally went on to coach the Australian national women's team, had been contacted by Hong Kong Rangers. They wanted him to track down a striker with a British passport, someone who would not need a work visa bearing in mind that Hong Kong was still under British rule at that time. The need was immediate and the chairman of the club happened to be in Sydney on business.

I was in the right place at the right time (being a striker, of course!), although I wasn't the first player to be approached. Here's where I got a bit lucky. Tom Sermanni was acquainted with another Scottish lad called Laurie McKinna who played for Blacktown City. Funnily enough, I faced McKinna and his team in my last game for Stanmore. Tom asked Laurie if he fancied the move to Hong Kong. Laurie turned it down. The reason was that he'd got married, had a steady job, and wasn't in a position to uproot. Laurie was then good enough to recommend me to Tom, talking about 'this young Scottish lad playing for Stanmore who did well against us.' Tom got hold of my number and phoned me direct. I was training with Wollongong by then and, bearing in mind the visa problems, I just went for it. But when I met the Hong Kong Rangers chairman, a Mr. Lam, at a Sydney hotel, things weren't quite so straightforward. He wavered about taking me. Mr. Lam said he wasn't sure as he knew very little about me, didn't know what kind of player I was, and only had the agent's word that I was a good one.

I put it to him that he was obviously a successful

businessman who must have been used to taking chances. I urged him to take a chance with me and promised to give him 100%. Unfortunately, he decided against. The brighter news came in another phone call – not quite as welcome as the first – from Tom Sermanni. The good news was that there was another Hong Kong team, called Kuitan, who were also on the look-out for a striker. I took their offer and went over to join them in January, 1993, which was halfway through their season. It was a landmark moment for me – my first full-time deal!

So farewell to Australia after just a few months. Well, I did say I would give it three! But I thought I would be heading back home at that point. Hong Kong had never been part of the Bullen masterplan. How to sum up the Aussies? Well, they are amazing people. We tend to have this picture of Aussie bums sitting on the beach tilting back tins of beer. Actually, they work very hard. It's so ingrained that people will get up at 5am to go to work. That way they get the best of both worlds. They lead a great outdoor lifestyle. Work hard and play hard sums it up best. As for the banter, well it was non-stop between us Brits and the Aussies. Being Scottish was actually a good thing. They'd say 'You hate the Poms as much as we do!'

Kuitan were struggling near the bottom of the league and I was one of several new boys brought in at the same time. We were an overnight success. By March, we were well clear of relegation. You'd have thought my bags would stay unpacked – for a while at least. But then, out of the blue, Kuitan transferred me a few weeks before the end of the season. I went to a team called Kitchee who wanted me because, whereas Kuitan were safe and had nothing to play for, they still had a chance in a couple of competitions. We got through to the Hong Kong Cup Final but ended up losing after I'd scored the first goal of the game.

Then yet another move. A new team called Golden came into the league. Yes, you've guessed it, I was to be one of their golden boys! They had a coach by the name of Simon Wong. He was fantastic to me, had a lot of faith in my ability, and helped me a great deal. The feeling must have been mutual as I ended up staying there for two years which was an eternity considering the nomadic state of my career up to that point, both in Scotland and abroad.

Golden were actually an electronics company who used the football team to heighten their profile. It was a very clever thing to do because an advert on television during a big game would cost a fortune. By running a team, Golden had their name plastered across the screen already. Maybe it is the next logical progression of the corporate takeover in Britain. Will we eventually be watching Manchester Vodafone United or whatever?

Apart from yours truly, Golden signed several Europeans to play in Hong Kong. There were Mike Duxbury (ex-Manchester United), former Wimbledon player Carlton Fairweather and a couple of Yugoslavs. All the clubs were full-time. So, as I say, Kuitan was actually my first full-time professional contract. I would get a decent wage plus some expenses. The rent was covered and I would also get a couple of free flights home. The biggest expense for someone based in Hong Kong was the living overheads, so not having to worry about paying rent resulted in virtually all the money after tax going into the player's pocket. In relative football terms it still wasn't a huge amount. But, hey, for me at the time it was a big deal. I was in dreamland!

Going to Australia in the first place had been the major emotional move for me and I had grown up very quickly there, so I wasn't worried at all about going to Hong Kong.

My time at Golden was fantastic. I really enjoyed it. One of the highlights was playing with a Bosnian striker by the name of Alen Bajkusa who came to the club a year after I'd joined. I was number seven, he wore eleven. We were such a hit that Golden brought out a mini hand-held computer and named it after us. It was called the 7-11. Amazing stuff. In Hong Kong there were also a chain of shops called 7-11. Everything seemed to click, including the computer sales. At one point, the club even wanted us to be in an advert for them. They ended up using a couple of actors instead. Probably a wise move! I should have held on to one of those computers as a keepsake, although I never did.

At that time in Hong Kong every team was allowed five foreign players. People often say to me that it must have been easy playing there because of my height advantage over the locals. But you'd often find that the spine of the team would be made up of foreign players. So the goalkeeper, central defenders, central midfielder and striker would usually be Europeans. As a striker, I would mostly be up against a foreign centre half of similar dimensions.

Mike Duxbury was an inspiration to me. Playing together in Hong Kong, I was impressed with his whole approach to the game. He joined Golden at the same time as me and we enjoyed a link-up which lasted for two years. He'd played at such a high level, having been at Old Trafford, but he never came across as flash or anything like that. I learnt a lot from him, just by the way he acted and talked about the game. He was a family man who would always have time to speak to the younger boys. Yet he also had time for a laugh and a joke. I remember thinking that if I ever got the chance to play at a higher level then I wanted to be like Mike Duxbury. Mike had more experience than our coach at the time and yet he'd let him get on with his job. Only now and then would he chip in with his views.

Being full-time made it feel like a step up from Australia. It was a totally different style of football. The major difference was a product of the humidity. Playing in such heat is not easy for the body, no matter how fit the individual concerned. In terms of quality, though, I'd say the teams were merely on a par with League Two in England. Only one side in the league had their own training ground. All the others trained in the same place in the middle of what was the Happy Valley horse and race track. That was incredibly bizarre. We'd be playing against a certain team on the forthcoming Saturday and during the week we'd be training on the same pitch as them. We could stand there and watch them practising their free-kick routines, as they could with us. The one good spin-off was that, off the pitch, you could become really good friends with a lot of players, not just your own team-mates.

The major step-up for me was playing for the Hong Kong select sides. A couple of different national teams would come over for the annual Carlsberg Cup in February which coincided with the Chinese New Year, and I was involved for three of the tournaments in the four or five years I was there. I got to play against the likes of Sweden, Colombia and the then Yugoslavia side. And I added some great shirts to my collection. What an education to play against some top stars. There was Sinisa Mihajlovic, who later played for Lazio and Inter Milan before managing Serbia. When we faced Sweden I came across the former Sheffield Wednesday right back Roland Nilsson. It was also the time when Henrik Larsson was just breaking through.

And I must mention, in the manner of a squirrel burying his nuts, that I also played against England. It was a team including Paul Gascoigne, David Platt and Paul Ince.

England won 1-0 with a goal from Les Ferdinand. But that's not why the game will be remembered. You may have heard something about it ...

5

Let Me Fill You In on the 'Dentist's Chair' ... I Was There!

It was a notorious night, still talked about to this day. And I was there. Not that anyone was too interested in me or my Hong Kong team-mates. This was the evening of the day we played England. Oh, and quite a bit of the following morning as well. I refer to the 'dentist's chair.' Yes, the infamous drinking escapade that made headlines around the world. And first of all let me tell you the dentist's chair was for real, an actual one as used in Hong Kong. Its previous life must have been quite eventful and yet it became famous for another purpose altogether.

I doubt anyone doesn't know what I'm talking about so I'll wind back a moment to our game against England. Had Terry Venables' team won 6-0 then probably not much would have been made about what followed. To win only 1-0 heaped criticism on the team in the build-up to Euro 96. And it could have been worse for England because I should have scored in that game. Can you imagine the indignity they would have felt then? I was through one-on-one with David Seaman after knocking Tony Adams off the ball. Seaman made a good save but I still think I ought to have buried that chance.

It was almost as shocking as our strip that day. We played in pink, England in grey. Anyway, the start of the Euros was a week away and Venables let the players out for the night. That alone is hardly controversial, nor is the fact that footballers tend to have a good time when let off the leash. And that is all they had really. Just a good time. Well, a very, very good time. A few shirts were ripped in horseplay but that was as far as it went in terms of any violence.

The fuse was lit when the England lads asked a few of us after the game about the best place to go for a night out. We mentioned our favourite haunt. It was a place popular with ex-pats and young Chinese. From outside you wouldn't know it was there. You approach it by going into an office block. There's a lift and you take it to the seventh floor. The lift door opens ... and you walk straight into a nightclub. Well, it was actually like a TGI Friday-type place that could turn itself into a nightclub later in the day. A good group of us went along to join the England lads. Now let's throw an extra ingredient into the mix – it was Paul Gascoigne's birthday as well. You get the drift of where we're going with this.

On a scale of one-to-ten for a footballers' night out I'd have to say this was an eight or a nine. But there was no trouble or anything, just high spirits in every meaning of the expression. Okay, some players might have got a little out of control but they were never going to get into a fight or cause trouble. I've seen far worse. You put any group of workers together – binmen, plumbers, anybody – and it wouldn't be much different on a good night out. None of the players were obnoxious with the other nightclubbers or anything of that nature. In fact, they might even have been too friendly as things turned out. Because it was the photographs taken that night of posing players that were inevitably sold to the newspapers. In that respect, the England lads were naïve.

At one stage they were ripping each other's shirts. That's really as bad as it got. It was in fun but it doesn't come across very well on film, and doesn't present a good image. And it gave scope for the stories that followed to run riot – even if the players really didn't. Don't forget there was a lot of negative publicity for England at that time as well. People were questioning why they'd gone to Hong Kong in the first place so close to a major tournament. Didn't turn out so bad, though, did it?

Ladies and gentlemen, time to introduce the star of the show. It was on a plinth in the corner of the dance floor. Doubtless it went on to enjoy the status of a statue, except this was the real thing as far as dentist's chairs are concerned, leather backed and adjustable. And I speak from the experience of having reclined there on one previous occasion. First you pay at the bar and then, when your turn comes, you sit down and the chair goes back. There's a spotlight on you just like in a surgery. A towel is put round your neck and across comes the barman in the role of the dentist. He has a bottle in each hand, one of vodka and one of lime. You get the drill! 'Open wide' and the contents of both bottles are poured down your throat until your mouth is overflowing.

Of the England party, only two or three players booked for an 'appointment.' As everyone knows, Gazza was one. But the most memorable incident which also involved him, was later that night. He was in a group of about a dozen in one corner having a raucous time. Then in walked Alan Shearer, Tim Flowers and a representative from the Umbro kit company. All three were stone cold sober. Gazza spotted the trio straight away and ran across towards them. He was really buzzing. Seeing the ripped shirts of all the players,

Shearer sensed trouble afoot. He stood behind Flowers who, as a goalkeeper, was a big guy, powerful and with big hands. Tim just grabbed Gazza's wrists and held tight as if to say 'no chance, pal.' Those three wanted to keep their smart T-shirts intact and they were having none of it.

It was a great night – and it went on all night. Obviously the coverage was bad for England at the time, just adding to the nation's sense of gloom and doom. But was it really so bad? Looking back, my view is that it was a terrific boost for team spirit because England went on to have a fantastic tournament. Just look at the Gazza celebration after he had scored a great goal in one of the first round games at Wembley. I was there but tend to forget who it was against. Oh, Scotland you say? Gazza re-enacted the dentist's chair escapade in his celebration of that goal. And suddenly the public loved it, not only forgiving the headlines but thinking the Hong Kong revelry had pulled the team together. England played some great stuff and went on to reach the semi-finals where they were beaten on penalties by Germany. So was it a bad night out or a good night out? I think it was a good one in every way.

6

Something In the Air ...

It's a funny thing. Whenever anybody came over to look me up in Hong Kong – family, friends etc – the first thing they mentioned was the smell of the place. Yet this was something I never noticed. They'd sniff the air in the streets and point it out. I suppose with so many people living in such a condensed area you are going to get the odd drainage problem. But it wasn't just that. There'd be the cooking smells from the many restaurants, the herbs on sale everywhere, and the many animal carcases hanging up outside shops. The different foods and spices all came together, not to mention the various homeopathic remedies on sale. Yet I never really detected the whiff others said that this combination produced. Maybe it's something to do with coming from Scotland!

I liked living in Hong Kong. I must have done to spend four years there. Besides, I found it to be one of the safest cities I've ever experienced. It was a 24-hour city and there was no threat at all. You could walk around at three o'clock in the morning and feel totally secure, unlike in some cities in the UK or, shall we say, Glasgow on a Saturday night. Yes, people would go out to have a good time and I saw loads of them drunk. But I never saw any violence apart from one solitary occasion.

This was so shocking it was like a scene from a Chinese movie. And from what I heard, it involved members of the criminal underworld known as the Triads. I came out one night from an ex-pats bar called 'Big Apple' to see a set-to in the street between two young Chinese guys. It was only a bit of a skirmish and was all over very quickly. Or so it seemed. Suddenly a running pitched battle kicked off. A couple of gangs had appeared from nowhere and it seemed to be a question of honour between them. This was serious stuff.

They were clubbing each other for about ten minutes. Blood was spilt and some were seriously hurt. I looked on in amazement. A couple of local lads mentioned the Triad thing and warned me not to get involved. Eventually the police arrived and let me tell you, they don't mess about. They put a stop to it very quickly. And let me stress as well that it was purely a tribal thing. If you weren't involved and stayed out of it you were in no danger whatsoever. Yes, it was like watching a movie scene.

As I say, I never noticed anything peculiar about the smell of the place. But there must have been something in the air. It was in Hong Kong that I got married! Her name was Kerry, she was a showgirl. Doesn't quite scan with the Barry Manilow song, does it? But there's some similarity in the lyrics. We met in the same nightclub that staged the England bash – although it was some time before the dentist's chair became a celebrity in its own right. This was Christmas Eve, 1995. Kerry, an English girl, was performing there. She'd been in Hong Kong for about three years, working as an aerobics instructor and also doing some dancing. She happened to be wearing tartan trousers, Rupert the Bear style, on the night we met and I think that was the topic of conversation that brought us together for a chat. It was the archetypal whirlwind romance. One thing led to another and we got married eleven months later.

The wedding took place in a church overlooking Happy Valley racetrack and I doubt Hong Kong or anywhere else has seen anything like this ceremony before or since. I had two best men, one English the other Portuguese, and managed to get them to wear kilts for the first time in their lives. What was more unusual was that Kerry's 'bridesmaids' were blokes. She had two men wearing trousers while my best men were in skirts! It was a fantastic occasion, much enjoyed by all. The church overlooked the ground where we and other teams trained. They all stopped to clap and cheer us during the picture session after the ceremony. My family came over and it was also an opportunity for my mum and dad to fly on to Australia. There, Mum was able to enjoy a reunion with her brother and sister.

Not talked about football much lately, have I? Well, there isn't too much left to speak about as far as Hong Kong is concerned. I joined the biggest club out there in 1997, but with hindsight, my move from Golden to South China was a mistake. Despite the name of my new club, it was still in HK, although this was the year of the handover of sovereignty from Britain back to China.

I suppose the move made sense in that South China had a 35,000 capacity stadium and could fill it for big games like cup finals. I saw it as an opportunity to advance my career. But there had been a portent that my future might lie elsewhere when I'd been approached shortly after the England game about an opportunity to play in Greece. This eventually came to pass but at the time of the original offer I was about to get married. It didn't seem the time to uproot so I moved to South China instead. The experience wasn't all bad. I got to play in friendlies against Chelsea and

Manchester United. This enabled me to add Frank Leboeuf's shirt to my collection and I also got one off the back of Steve Clarke who was glad to present it to me knowing I was a fellow Scot.

South China lasted all of six months. I was in and out of the team, not enjoying it. But it turned out that, figuratively speaking, I still had a passport to Greece in my back pocket. Based in Hong Kong was a Greek guy called Stavros Papadopoulos. That undersells him a bit. He's actually a very rich man, one of the wealthiest in Greece. His business was diamond and emerald mining in Brazil, though its head office was in HK. Stavros watched a lot of the local football which actually featured many Brazilian players. Someone representing him had approached three of us – including a Brazilian and a Portuguese – after the England game on behalf of his links with clubs in Greece. Eventually all three of us ended up going out there. We left Hong Kong in December, 1997.

Kerry was beginning to get itchy feet as well, although the move was a lot easier from my point of view than her's. Working in a football environment, I would get much more interaction than her in terms of learning the language and adapting to the culture. If I was tied down to a two-year contract then effectively so was she. While she was a traveller by nature, previously she'd been able to up sticks and go somewhere else if things didn't suit her. This time she was captive to an extent.

The club I joined was Kalamata in the top division in Greece. Mr. Papadopoulos was the chairman and the owner. Kalamata itself was a fantastic place, right on the Mediterranean and the sort of resort you'd gladly visit on holiday. The football side of things was also quite pleasant. As before, I threw myself into socialising with the other players. You had to make an effort. It was the only way to get accepted and also to learn the language. The other players appreciated you joining in. Besides, it would have been a cop out for Kerry and myself to just spend our time sitting in cafes beside the Med.

We even took lessons in Greek, paid for by ourselves and not by the club. I was only there a couple of years but I got the hang of it. I'd be able to hold conversations in Greek and even now, if I'm out there on holiday, I can soon pick it up again. Of course, it's Greek with a Scottish accent. But I do think people understand me better out there than they do in England! Maybe there's a message in that somewhere.

On a more serious level, I do think it's vitally important for players to put cultural and even language differences to one side when they join clubs that are foreign to them. People in Sheffield talk about a divided Hillsborough dressing room the last time Wednesday had some really big stars in their team. This was in the mid-to-late 1990s, the era of the two great Italians, Paolo Di Canio and Benito Carbone. So I was struck recently to read a national newspaper feature on Carbone in which he openly admitted not 'joining in' and that it was a mistake on his part.

In the Daily Mail article, Carbone is quoted: 'It became two Italians on one side, and the English players on the other. It was partly my fault. I should have tried harder to mix with the others. The problem was that they would invite me for a pint, but I didn't drink. I have always been teetotal, so I never joined them. That's where I went wrong. If I could rewind, I would go with them, order a coke and laugh at any stick about being a lightweight. That way, we would have got on. It's the English mentality to go for a pint and I should have realised.'

That, for me, perfectly sums up why I have always felt

players should make an effort to come together off the pitch because in my experience there is always a benefit on the field when that happens. It was fascinating to read Carbone's comments and full marks to him for his honesty.

Anyway, Kalamata's manager at the time the move was mooted was the great Brazilian Jairzinho, who scored in every game when his country won the World Cup in 1970. Unfortunately, I never had the chance to work with him. Jairzinho was sacked just before the three of us joined Kalamata. A Greek guy took over and we simply weren't his pick, we were the chairman's choice. You could sense he didn't take to the other two lads, although I didn't feel that myself. My Portuguese pal was only offered a six-month contract which was then paid up as he left after only two weeks. The Brazilian and myself both had two-year deals. He was very much on the fringe of things whereas I felt involved. Of course, living out of a suitcase in a hotel didn't help. Despite this, the training went well and slowly we settled in. My debut was against OFI Crete, coming on for the second half in a 1-1 draw, and then I started the next game. It was a local derby and I scored the equaliser in another draw. That was enough to get me started with both my team-mates and the fans.

As I say, things were harder for Kerry. Initially she wasn't working and learning the language was the barrier to getting any sort of job. This was another very good reason why we both took lessons. Kerry had a lot of spare time and this proved to be a blessing in the end. They do say necessity is the mother of invention. She started painting lovely pictures that helped fill the walls of our empty apartment. Pretty soon a few of my team-mates took to admiring her work and wanted to get their hands on some of it. Eventually some of the local cafes also got interested and painting became a business for her, snowballing to the point where she was able to continue it when we eventually returned to Britain.

Kerry had to put her art work on the back burner for a while when we had kids but she is back into it now. Bizarrely, when I moved to Sheffield I spotted a picture that looked like one of Kerry's but without her customary signature. I took a photo of it on my phone and sent it to her in Scotland. She immediately recognised it as one of her own. Kerry said she hadn't signed it because she didn't like it! But somebody obviously did and it found its way to Sheffield. Just as I did ... but that's a story for later.

In my first half-season with Kalamata we were relegated. In the second we came right back up and things were good. But at the beginning of the following season I tore a muscle in one knee and began to drift out of the picture. I got to the point where I was thinking 'Do they actually want me here?'

It was also the start of me drifting back in the positional sense. I found myself playing as a wing-back. That would change back again to striker when I made my next move, a return to Scotland. For once, a little forward planning was involved. While we were in Greece, my mum had bought a house for us in Edinburgh. It was intended as an investment for the future, but it also gave us a place to go.

Kerry wasn't unhappy in Greece but I wouldn't say she was at her happiest either. She'd tell you all about that if you asked! Despite it all, there was never any question of me not seeing out the contract. We were both determined to give it a go. At the end of the two years, Kerry was ready for moving and I was feeling a bit of friction at the club.

Due to the chairman's overbearing influence we had gone through four or five coaches in my time at Kalamata.

They were often just puppets for him as well. He would frequently phone them up and tell them what team to put out. While that has become increasingly prevalent in the game, it just doesn't feel right to me. There were no talks about a new contract so in mid-December, 1999 we made up our minds to leave and return to the UK.

7

Dunroamin? Well, Dunfermline Anyway (Again)

So here I am heading back to dear old Blighty. But don't furl me up the white flag of surrender. In the end, that was some overseas campaign I fought! Don't forget that when I made that tearful farewell from Scotland I was intending to give it just three months in Australia. That's if my resolve lasted that long. *Just* three months? That's still quite a stretch for a young guy at 21. And I ended up staying away for seven whole years! So I look back with pride at that time in my life. I stuck at it and can savour experiences that many will never contemplate, let alone pursue. I did a lot of growing up in that time, too, of course. It was a better man – and player – who returned to these shores and I think my subsequent career proved that.

But, in a sense, I wasn't 'coming back' at all. The decision was about returning to Britain. Not Scotland. It was in England that I wanted to play next and pick up my career. Why? Well, for starters I feared I was written off north of the border. I've already mentioned how everybody knows everybody up there. The word would have gone round about my various trials and tribulations, the struggle to settle with one club and to make a full-time career of the

46

game. Not that I questioned my ability to do so, this was just the view of me taken by others. Besides, I fancied playing in England. There's no trainspotter in me. I wasn't trying to clock up some sort of record for clubs and countries. It just seemed to me that England was my best shot.

With Scotland being a closed book offering no second chance – or so I thought – here's what I decided to do. Yes, I spoke to a fellow Scot, of course! While still in Greece I talked to Billy Kirkwood who was then coaching in Hong Kong. Billy, who subsequently moved to Dundee, fixed me up with an agent by the name of Blair Morgan. Through Blair a deal was organised for me at Walsall. They invited me along to training and offered a five-day trial just before Christmas. You see, I always do my shopping late!

Unfortunately, my contract in Greece did not expire officially until the end of the month. What didn't help either, was that there was a bit of antagonism between us. The animosity meant that they wouldn't sanction the international clearance required for me to play in competitive games, even including the reserves, until the contract finished on December 31st.

Here's where fate took another twist. Maybe the hold-up worked well for me in the long run, as you'll see. But at the time it was very frustrating. There was nothing Walsall could do and so they sent me back up to Scotland for the festive period with a request to return in January when they would look at me in a couple of games. In the meantime, agent Blair arranged for me to keep up my fitness by training with Dunfermline, my first club, while I was in Scotland for a couple of weeks. There was no hidden agenda whatsoever and I just expected to be training with the kids. However, coaches Jimmy Calderwood and Jimmy Nicholl were exceptionally good to me. To my surprise, I was included in the first-team activities.

Coinciding with this, Dunfermline suffered a striker crisis. One forward had gone to Kilmarnock on loan and another, Owen Coyle (later to become a high-profile manager at Burnley and Bolton) was sent off, receiving a two-match ban. I'd played in a couple of informal behind-closed-doors matches. These were against Rangers and Dundee United – and I scored in both. You can see where this is heading. My good showing and Dunfermline's lack of strikers meant that I was offered a contract until the end of the season. I never went back to Walsall and instead scored seven goals in 11 games for Dunfermline that season.

I was 29 when I returned to East End Park in 2000. I'd been 18 when I left the first time. That just shows that the years that might have been considered to be my peak time as a footballer had been spent on my travels. But they hadn't passed me by. Not yet. The best, most enjoyable phase of my career was yet to come. And don't forget that Dunfermline were regular members of the Scottish Premier League at that time. They'd been fleetingly relegated but had just returned at the first time of asking when I rejoined them.

And my remaining four years of this spell in Fife were to be spent in the top flight. This was also to be the period that would see a centre-forward become a centre-half – and most other positions in between. You'd think at nearly 30 it would be too late to teach the proverbial old dog some new tricks. This old dog proved to be quite a quick learner. Just as well, too. He'd have been pretty much down at heel if he hadn't.

As I said, things went quite well for me on my restart with The Pars. Better than par for the course actually. Ouch! I earned a longer deal to replace the short-term contract and was feeling fairly settled back in Scotland. Things went well for the first year, in fact. But you can never look too far ahead in this game and I was in for a nasty surprise. Manager Jimmy Calderwood slapped me on the transfer list. This came totally out of the blue and the reason was that he wanted to bring in some more of his own players.

How players react to that kind of blow can vary according to circumstance. Experience is also a factor and I was old enough to handle it. Not that I could handle every blow to my pride – as you'll see in the next chapter. In this instance, I took a deep breath and counted to ten. What helped was that I had a year remaining on my contract. So, in the worst case scenario, I would be able to pay the mortgage for another twelve months. Yes, footballers at my level at that time still had to think like that. As they do to this day at many levels of the game outside of the top echelons.

There are times when you think you might have found a way back into the manager's plans. Oddly enough, one of those was when we beat Sheffield Wednesday 3-1 in a pre-season friendly in July, 2001. I scored one of the goals and set up another. My performance playing as a wing-back became a talking point in the media. Injuries had reduced Calderwood's options in that position and he admitted after the game that I could yet earn an extended stay at East End Park.

Calderwood told the press: 'Lee's got pace, he's strong and he can come in at the back post as well. He's a great lad. Obviously his first choice is at centre forward and he's at an age now where he needs to play. Things could change. I don't want to lose him and he never lets you down. You never know in football.'

I felt there was no point in sulking or stirring up trouble because it wouldn't do me any good in the long run. I'd be better off working hard in the hope of changing the manager's mind. Then I could get myself in the shop window of the first team rather than playing in the reserves. During this unsettled time I went for a trial at Luton Town, a club with a top-flight history who were then trying to battle back up from the fourth tier under the management of Joe Kinnear and his assistant Mick Harford.

I was listed as A.N.Other in a practice game but the word was out that Luton were looking at a striker. A bit of speculation inevitably followed and I heard that some fans thought I was Luke Beckett who was a prolific marksman around the lower divisions at that time. Probably wishful thinking on their part. What they were actually getting, or nearly got, was a guy who by this time was playing as a wing-back up in Scotland.

In fact, I hadn't played as a striker for three or four months. Despite this, Luton put me up front in a reserve game and I scored in a 3-3 draw with Queens Park Rangers. So I was feeling reasonably confident when I went to see the manager during training the next day. He said I'd done pretty well and made me an offer. But it was not what I wanted. I'd been looking for a fresh start somewhere and was attracted to the idea of playing in England. What was actually on the table was a three-month loan deal. With a wife and also, by this time, a son back home in Edinburgh, it had to be something more concrete than that if we were to uproot the family. And there was no way I could commute over that distance. I told Luton I'd think about the offer. In reality, I went back up the road to Scotland knowing I would not be turning around.

Things somehow took care of themselves from that point. I always felt in a position where I was continually having to prove myself to Jimmy Calderwood. Maybe that's no bad thing in a way because it means you can never rest on your laurels. In the end, he took me off the transfer list and offered a new two-year contract which I gladly accepted. Jimmy got my respect for that. There is no going back with some managers once their minds are made up. He was big enough to reconsider and his decision indicated an acknowledgment that maybe he'd made the wrong call in the first place. I had won him over by working my way slowly but surely into the first team. I played at right wing-back and then in a more traditional right back role.

Events had finally turned my way in the autumn of 2001. Calderwood joked at the time that he'd bowed to the pressure of letters and emails calling for me to get a new deal. He told the club's website: 'I think Bully keeps sending them himself! The way he was playing, if someone had come in for him, I was in a dilemma. Circumstances change every day in football. The lad's done well, not only in his own position, centre forward, but also on the right side – and we have a problem on that side. Maybe he can help us solve that problem. As I've said before, everyone thinks the world of him. It's not only the supporters but the players too. He's a great lad to have in the group.'

Nice words which I appreciated at the time. And nice to be called 'lad' as well!

Reflecting on my time at East End Park, I particularly enjoyed a spell up front alongside Stevie Crawford, a Scotland international who was still involved with the national side. There was a great understanding between us. Not that this didn't stop us squaring up to each other at the end of one game. This was during a Cup replay at Aberdeen after we'd conceded a late penalty that almost cost us victory.

It was Stevie giving the ball away that led to my centre back partner bringing somebody down in the box. I gave

Stevie a mouthful and he gave me one back. Considering we played at opposite ends of the park that night, we must have walked 30 odd yards to confront each other. And it's fair to say we almost came to blows. I felt we'd given the ball away too cheaply and we were at each other's throats. But it blew over quickly and we were both apologetic afterwards.

Besides, we held on to the lead and all it really showed was how much we wanted to win the game. The player who took my place alongside Stevie was Craig Brewster, who went on to become one of my best friends in the game. Craig turned pro very late but became a much respected figure, going on to manage Dundee United among others. He looked after himself so well that he played on throughout his thirties. Although Craig isn't much older than me, he's someone I've always looked up to. And if ever I become a manager, he's the type of player I will want in my team.

I mentioned my up and down relationship with Jimmy Calderwood. It was never more down than at the end of my final season at East End Park. And it was on the rebound from that downer that I enjoyed the biggest upper. Safety belts on – this is a real rollercoaster ride!

8

'You're Not Playing in the Cup Final'

I wasn't the first player to be left out of a cup final and I won't be the last. Somehow these big occasions often throw up stories of heartbreak for some unfortunate individual even before a ball is kicked.

Let me tell you, those unfortunate individuals find something else to kick instead. I know I certainly did! And no, I don't keep a cat! Usually the drama involves a player who expects to play and is also expected to play by everyone else. However, the regularity with which this sort of scenario unfolds is no consolation whatsoever when the guy at the centre of it all happens to be you. It's hard to describe but I'll do my best from the benefit, if that's the right word, of bitter experience.

For all the highs and lows in the game (and I was to sample my biggest one of each in the space of a year) you never actually learn to cope with either of these extremes. How can you? Win one week, lose the next. Elation and despair is part of the life we lead. But if we ever got used to it and came to accept it as 'a way of life' then that would be the time when we didn't care anymore. And we could no longer do our jobs. It's a vicious circle, in effect. So I make no apologies for my reaction to the news Jimmy Calderwood gave me in the spring of 2004.

It was the climax to a great season for Dunfermline which still promised so much. We finished fourth in the league as well as reaching the final of the Scottish Cup for the first time in 36 years. The Pars had been winners of the trophy back in 1968, as they had been in 1961. Could we bring the cup back to East End Park for the third time in the club's history?

In the wake of our semi-final win over Inverness Caledonian Thistle, I played in all five league matches in the lead up to the big day at Hampden Park. I made 35 appearances that campaign, rounding off to 150 for Dunfermline. And there was an extra emotional element that helped tip me over the edge when the fateful news arrived. I already knew that the final would be my swansong for the club after nearly four-and-a-half years there.

Celtic were to be our opponents. Yes, it could only be one of two! But we had no reason to fear Martin O'Neill's team. We'd pulled off a shock result by beating them 2-1 at Parkhead just a couple of weeks before the final. Showing my versatility and hopefully my value to the team, I'd taken a left-side role that day. Players know when they've played well and they know when they've played badly. I was delighted with my performance in that game. I set up one of the goals and was extremely happy.

It left us with three more games between the Celtic victory and the all-important re-match at Hampden. To be honest, we weren't quite at our best in those, none of us were. Several of the team held their hands up and admitted they could have done better after we lost at Hearts the following week. Then came a 3-2 defeat at Dundee United three days later, although I scored one of our goals.

I genuinely thought I had done enough to secure my place in the team for the final. I think everyone did. Then, a couple of days before the game, Jimmy Calderwood dropped his bombshell on me. We'd just been training on the Astroturf pitch at the stadium and everyone was still around. I suspected nothing out of the ordinary. Then the gaffer called me through to his office. His message was blunt, although I suppose there's no easy way to deliver this sort of stuff.

'It's not good news – I'm not going to start you in the cup final,' he said. One word and one word only popped out of my gaping mouth: 'Why?' The gaffer told me that he thought my standards had dropped over the previous couple of games and that he was putting me on the bench. What? Why me? I felt fully entitled to take it personally, asking if I was the only one whose standards had supposedly dropped. After all, several players had admitted as much. And I was the only one who was actually dropped. I was dumbfounded. I just couldn't take it in.

People talk about the red mist coming down and that is certainly the right colour for it. I was like a raging bull. I charged back into the changing rooms and then around the corner into the shower area. I swore at the top of my voice and kicked the walls in frustration. I was absolutely gutted, almost in tears, but trembling with anger too. The club captain, Scott 'Nipper' Thomson, poked his head in to see what the commotion was about. I was still fighting to get my emotions together. He asked what was wrong and I told him I'd been dropped. There was a dumbfounded reaction. He didn't seem to believe it either but clearly didn't know what to say. There are no words that can heal in that situation, as I know only too well having been on both sides of the fence. He offered me his commiserations and quickly left me to it, understandably so. I sat there in a pool of misery. The biggest game of my life had been snatched away from me.

Try picking yourself up from something like that. Normally, the downers are after a game if you've lost. This was far worse than any defeat. And my mood contrasted so sharply with everything going on around me – the excitement, the anticipation. Instead of sharing in that, I was absolutely devastated. I'm usually the type of guy who doesn't let things affect him. I've already described how I reacted to being slapped on the transfer list. My inclination to setbacks is to get my head down and work even harder. But this was different. The disappointment really got to me. And I spent two days feeling so down, as low as I've ever felt.

Then, on the day of the game, I realised that it was not all about me. I had to pick myself up for the sake of the players and the fans. This was a huge occasion for them. It wasn't doing my team-mates any good to see me moping around and tripping up over my bottom lip. They knew only too well of my disappointment and heartbreak but it was time to get behind them, to help if I could. So I started to approach things a little differently. Above all, I was determined not to let my emotions show. Besides, it could have been worse. I was named as a substitute and anything could happen. You never know if someone might get injured early on and I had to be ready to take my chance if that happened.

Excitement overcame depression as our coach turned in towards Hampden Park. There must have been about 15,000 Dunfermline fans outside the stadium. I'd never seen so many people decked out in the Pars' black-and-white strip, all stacked up along the banking that adjoined the ground. They all stood up to cheer our arrival and that was great. It gave me a few butterflies and helped to focus my mind again. Now I could start treating it as a normal game ... in a manner of speaking.

We went out onto the pitch and warmed up with everyone getting on with their normal preparations for a game. At that point, I thought my personal anguish was behind me. But it hit me again just before kick-off. There were the starting eleven out on the pitch doing the VIP bit, shaking hands, then standing with the national anthem playing. And there was me, sat watching it all from the bench. That was a real downer. I was gutted all over again. And there was no doubt in my mind that I should have been out there starting the game.

A goal from Andrius Skerla just before half-time saw us ahead at the break. Could we hold our shock lead? Could I help us do that if the opportunity arose? And it did. Well, very nearly. I was summoned for a holding operation and we were still leading 1-0 as I warmed up on the touchline, confident of helping us pull off an incredible victory. But just as I was getting changed, Henrik Larsson equalised for Celtic in the 58th minute. I still came on, replacing Gary Dempsey and slotting in at right wing-back. It meant action for me at both ends. From making a clearance off our goal-line, I suddenly had a chance to put us 2-1 up. But my shot was blocked by Stanislav Varga and went out for a corner. It was to be Larsson's day. The Swede struck again in the 71st minute before Stilian Petrov wrapped up Celtic's victory.

So all the headlines revolved around Larsson's heroics in his last competitive game for Celtic. My farewell to Dunfermline went by the board. Not that I begrudge the Swede his glory. He was a sensational goalscorer. But I do still wonder if our gaffer picked the right team that day, certainly in regard to myself. One online report on the game actually said: 'Jimmy Calderwood's decision to pick a side full of footballers instead of trying to match Celtic's physical presence appeared to have backfired.' I think there's something in that, regardless of the self-interest.

Not that this was uppermost among the many emotions swirling inside my head during the walk-round after the final whistle. The main feeling was one of pride. I was extremely proud of what we achieved with that squad of players at Dunfermline. We improved year on year. There was promotion, survival in the Premier League, getting into the top six, then the top five and finally the top four, culminating in the cup final and qualification for the UEFA Cup. I look back with great satisfaction on the part I played and with fond memories of our terrific team spirit. We were a great group of players with a small but very loyal band of supporters.

Like the saying goes, all good things come to an end. Under Jimmy Calderwood it was obvious that I was going to be a bit-part player at best. In the event, he moved on to Aberdeen, although my mind was already made up that I had to leave as well. I had my ups and downs with Jimmy and I still think he was wrong to leave me out. But we do speak occasionally and the decision is in the past. There's nothing personal about it, which is the way it should be.

I was 33 by the time my Dunfermline days ended, but I'd had a good season and there was no shortage of interest in this versatile veteran (well, I'd dispute the second bit but it just sounds good!). Two Scottish clubs came in with offers of two-year contracts. Then there was a certain interest from an English club …

9

Hi-Ho Sheffield Wednesday!

We came in with the *Candyman* but there's another song that never fails to stir me. It made the charts four years before I was born and is one of those timeless hits that make you feel good whenever you hear it played – not least at three o'clock on a Saturday afternoon.

Jeff Beck's *Hi-Ho Silver Lining*, a rousing disco number from 1967, was the soundtrack to the best years of my career. It's just brilliant as a football song providing your club has the right number of syllables in its name. Shef-field Wednes-day scans beautifully. It's the perfect fit – just like my move to Hillsborough in the summer of 2004.

Up to then, it seemed likeliest I would stay in Scotland. Livingston and Motherwell came in with decent offers, so I was not short of choice. Then, out of the blue, Sheffield Wednesday came in for me. Just the name alone is a huge selling point. As you know, I hankered after a taste of English football having dabbled with the likes of Walsall and Luton. Wednesday were in a different league. Well, not strictly true in real terms as the Owls were down in the third tier after years of gradual decline. But this was a club with huge support, history and tradition.

I sat down and talked over the move with Kerry but to be honest it was a no-brainer for me. I'd always fancied playing in England and, although I hadn't followed Wednesday's fortunes since their relegation from the Premier League in 2000, the size of the club dictated all my thinking. Their interest was very exciting for me. And I have to admit I pursued it with a lot of self-interest from the point of view of my family. Here was a dilemma. We were settled in Scotland with kids aged three and one. Kerry was not a typical footballer's wife. She had her friends in Edinburgh, she was working there. As was the case from the day we met, Kerry had her own life and her own interests. When it came down to decision time I was selfish in a way. Certain opportunities really are once-in-a-lifetime, if you'll forgive the old cliché. This was nothing to do with money. There was no real gain or loss in moving to Hillsborough. It was purely about the size of the club. Over recent years, Wednesday have signed many a player who would have rejected similar terms from elsewhere. The place has pulling power.

There were a few twists and turns in my case, though. Story of my life! A two-year offer was halved to one because of a mix-up over my age. Bear in mind I was 33 by this time. Security for a couple of seasons is pretty good at that stage of your career and I could have had that in Scotland. Still, I took the gamble of coming south. That's the pulling power I was referring to just now. Wednesday's chief scout, Peter Eustace, had watched me a couple of times. After that, the assistant manager Colin West had taken a look. They invited me down to Sheffield to check out the place. To say the very least, it was totally different to anything I'd experienced. Even though part of the ground dates back 50 years, Hillsborough is a stadium that makes an instant impression on visitors. It's what you might call grand. Another departure for me was that the club had a separate training ground.

Naturally the club sold itself and I headed back up the road with my mind pretty well made up. It wasn't until my agent phoned me that I realised Wednesday were offering only a one-year deal and not the two I'd expected. They'd made a mistake over my age, thinking I was a couple of years younger. That's what caused a bit of deliberation over the move, nothing else.

Chris Turner, the Wednesday manager of the time, takes up the story …

'Lee fitted our mould. We'd liked what we'd seen of him playing for Dunfermline – his ability, size, mobility and strength. We also knew he could play in a number of positions, having watched him playing left wing-back on one occasion. It was as a right back that we signed Lee, having contacted his agent, and started negotiations quite early in the summer.

'We knew we were getting a versatile player but one of the biggest things we heard about Lee was how good a professional he was. And quite right too. We recognised that he was captaincy material. Although we'd already signed Chris Marsden and installed him as skipper, it was good to have Lee as another talker on the pitch and in the dressing room.

'When we found out he was 33, having originally been told by the chief scout that he was 31, I sat down with Lee. We'd initially told his agent we would sign him on a two-year deal. I explained to Lee that I'd spoken to our directors and we were a little concerned about his age. That was because we'd had a history of signing players and seeing them getting injured. But I did say to Lee that if he was doing well by Christmas or New Year, then we would rip up the contract and make it two years. Lee could easily have said that he was only prepared to sign for two, but he said 'okay, that's not a problem.'

'We had one or two injuries early on in the season and Lee did outstandingly well for us at centre-back. He was a very fit lad for his age. His attitude also stood out. You have to look at his lifestyle and training methods. All credit to Lee for looking after himself so well.'

My grateful thanks to Chris Turner for that contribution and also for the chance he gave me at Hillsborough. My only regret about what turned out to be a memorable and magical first season in England is that the manager who signed me wasn't around to enjoy that success. But, as a Wednesday supporter himself, he's never been bitter about that. And, as much as you have to give Chris credit for assembling the team that got us promotion, you have to give the chairman, Dave Allen, his due for making a change that worked.

You also have to remember the politics of the time. And politics were never far removed from Hillsborough in that era of the club's history. When I arrived Ken Bates was making a concerted attempt to take over the club. Chris was in the middle of the battleground as manager. I was very glad Bates did not succeed as he would have brought a lot of uncertainty. But there was huge pressure on the board to find an alternative way forward and when results dipped with a new team still in the settling process, a change was made in the management. I owe Chris a massive debt of gratitude for his faith in me. We will never know whether the same success would have come if he had stayed in charge. The chairman made a difficult decision in what he felt were the best interests of the club and it came off for all concerned.

Sheffield Wednesday was a whole new world to me, a different entity to any of the clubs I'd played for previously. Growing up I hadn't particularly followed them. Kenny

Dalglish was my hero and therefore Liverpool were my team in England, but I'd always been aware of Wednesday. I remembered them being a top team with household names such as Chris Waddle and David Hirst. The ground was a theatre of dreams just by itself. I was so struck by it when Chris Turner first showed me round the place. It didn't matter that League One football was being played there. This was an exciting opportunity for somebody aged 33. Wednesday's plight gave me a chance I wouldn't have had in other circumstances. And it would be so apt to say that every cloud has a silver lining.

First up came the most bizarre pre-season trip in all my long experience. We went to Ibiza. Now that's normally the place you head to for an end-of-season knees-up, not for the business of hard preparation. But it certainly achieved the objective of bringing a new squad together. It was, shall we say, a team-building trip.

First of all, it was about hard work – but play did kind of work its way into it! Chris Turner's thinking was spot on. He felt that after a lot of upheaval in the squad with a dozen or so leaving and new arrivals in double figures, he needed to create a feeling of togetherness. And that unity had to be in place quickly. I think he knew that if we didn't hit the ground running then he'd be out of a job.

It was bloody hot for training in Ibiza where we were also involved in a tournament that included Watford and Preston. We ended up being beaten by Watford on penalties in the final. That was more than respectable and most of our pre-season results were good, suggesting a successful season. What I remember most are the characters in that squad. Striker Lee Peacock, who'd arrived from Bristol City, was the most outgoing, loud, brash personality you could find anywhere. And yet deep inside I thought he was quite a shy person. Work that one out! Now put Lee into the same mix as Guy Branston. Literally – what a Guy! He's a much-travelled centre half and there's not a bigger character in the game. Above all, he's a lovely bloke. For all the fact that he's had his disciplinary problems and all his suspensions, managers will always want players like Guy. He'll fight tooth and nail for his team-mates. Definitely the bloke you want in the trenches with you.

Besides the personality and experience in that dressing room, we also had great talent. This is thanks once again to the manager of the time. Look at two more of those signings he made that summer, winger Chris Brunt and midfielder Glenn Whelan. Both have gone on to careers in the Premiership. Then there was another wide man, Jon-Paul McGovern, picked up from Livingston in Scotland. JP, Glenn, goalkeeper David Lucas and myself shared apartments on the outskirts of the city. We were the four musketeers. Then there was Paul Heckingbottom, a left back of sharp humour and high intellect. I found him to be a very funny guy who had the answer to anything. The mixture included former Wolves striker Adam Proudlock, a very talented player who just seemed to have a screw loose somewhere. He lived life to the full, shall we say.

Steadying it all off was Chris Marsden, a former top player with Southampton among others. Chris was also a Wednesdayite. Considering he'd been there and done it, he was the natural choice for captain. On top of his enduring quality as a player, he was a leaning post for a lot of the lads. Chris had to give up the game through injury that season, which was a heavy loss for us.

I knew pretty quickly that I'd joined a good group. There was no 'them and us,' no big-time Charlies. Chris had brought together a lot of genuine footballers, hungry to do well for a big club and the biggest club that most of us had played for. Oh, and we also had a former Rangers striker in Steve MacLean and an emerging young defender, Richard Wood. Quite a collection.

That's quite a build-up to a season, isn't it? A real big build-up from me. And what happened? The balloon went pop in our first game. We went out full of confidence on the first day of the season against Colchester at Hillsborough and somehow lost 3-0. The scoreline was misleading to say the least. We played some great stuff at times and our visitors scored with every opportunity they got. But from being so high we ended up being well and truly stuffed. I wondered what was going through the head of the manager and also the chairman, Dave Allen.

But this was the Wednesday way. Always the hard way for us. The players and fans were stunned. No-one could understand it. During that 90 minutes we saw both sides of a crowd that can work either for you or against you. Hillsborough is a hostile place with fans desperate for success. But I've seen the other side of this. Both in my time and later – for instance, attending the win-for-promotion home game against Wycombe in 2012. I can vouch for the fact that there is no greater sense of support than at Hillsborough when things are going well. There is nothing better. As we shall discover …

10

'You're Just a Striker Playing at the Back'

I've mentioned more than once how keen I was to play in England. Even with all my experience, it proved to be a rude awakening. We'd had a great pre-season but I'd not been truly aware of the standard in League One. There were some good players at that level and also a variety of tactical play in evidence from resourceful managers. Some teams were direct and others liked to get the ball down. Every game was also a physical battle and this applied to Sheffield Wednesday more than most because we were the biggest scalp, the ones everybody wanted to beat. Chris Turner was looking to succeed with a footballing style and he'd put Chris Marsden at the centre of things as our orchestrator.

We recovered quickly from the let down of opening day. Three days later we won 2-1 at Blackpool where I switched flanks to left back and scored my first goal for the club. It was a great volley, even if I say so myself! Then we triumphed 4-2 down at Torquay and confirmed what seemed to be a winning groove by edging out Huddersfield 1-0 at Hillsborough. After that, quite inexplicably, the wheels came off in a five match win-less run that cost Chris his job. I'm still quite puzzled as to what went wrong because the platform had seemed to be set.

A 4-2 crash at Tranmere was followed by a disappointing 1-1 draw at home to Oldham whose goal was scored by a certain Jermaine Johnson. JJ, later to become a Hillsborough hero, was on loan with Oldham from Bolton at the time. He showed in the manner of his goal that once he escapes a defence there is just no stopping a player of his extreme pace. There followed a goalless home game with Luton and a 1-1 draw at Walsall.

Another thing I'd not been aware of when I joined the club was the political uncertainty surrounding it. The Bates takeover issue barely got a mention in the dressing room but it didn't take me long to figure it all out. Looking back, I'm glad I had the experience both to do that and to be able to deal with it when questions were asked by reporters. This applied particularly later in the season when I became skipper after Chris Marsden retired. You have to be cute or certain questions will catch you off guard. The golden rule is not to get involved in whatever might be happening behind the scenes and concentrate on your job of playing.

But maybe the issues in the background did play a part in what happened next. A 1-0 home defeat to Bournemouth on September 18th left us in 14th place and led to Chris being sacked that very night. I know it wasn't an easy decision for Dave Allen who was under pressure from outside influences. Would Chris still have taken us up? Who can say? But the majority of the team promoted under Paul Sturrock were Chris's players. That said, we played a different way under Paul and his loan signing of Kenwyne Jones was a masterstroke, as we shall see.

Personally, I was very sad to see Chris leave. He came into the ground next day to say goodbye to the players and he looked a broken man, so disappointed. I don't think it really came as a surprise to him but news like that is a blow whether you are expecting it or not. Don't forget Chris's feeling for the club, having supported the team and then played in goal the last time Wednesday won a major trophy in beating Manchester United to lift the 1991 League Cup.

There was a sense of despondency in the changing room and also uncertainty. Every player feels the same way when a manager leaves. Sometimes there are those who are out of the picture who might welcome a change but that wasn't the case with Chris. We were already a tight-knit group and the manager was well supported. The next guy might come in and think you are a waste of space. In my case, Chris was the very first manager at this sort of level who I thought had 100% faith in me. He gave me a sense of confidence and belonging. And he even asked my opinion on things which is something I'd never known before. I felt I didn't have to continually prove myself to him and he had my immediate respect. Yes, he was the first manager who I felt trusted me as a player AND a person. Chris looked to the older ones in the dressing room and any manager needs support from his senior players.

Paul Sturrock swiftly emerged as our new boss and was appointed within five days, based in part on a firm recommendation from Chris himself. I had something in common with Sturrock as a fellow Scot but apart from having followed his career, I didn't know him at all. Neither did most of the other lads. What I did know was that Paul was a brilliant footballer and had a great CV as a manager.

As a striker for Dundee United he'd scored 109 goals in 385 appearances, besides boasting 20 caps and three goals for Scotland. As a manager, he'd won promotion at St. Johnstone in 1997 and then, following a less than happy return to Dundee United, Sturrock went to the other end of

Britain to take charge of Plymouth Argyle. There he was a sensational success for a club that had hit the lowest point in its history. Under Paul, they won promotion from the bottom tier in 2003, amassing a record 102 points. Argyle were firmly on course for a second successive promotion when he was lured to Southampton in March, 2004. Saints were a particularly difficult club to manage in that era and Paul's reign lasted a mere five months before he left by 'mutual consent.' So it was that a boss, supremely well qualified for the challenge Wednesday presented. was readily available.

Paul was very different in style and personality to Chris, but he certainly deserved the opportunity. It also has to be said that it takes a big man to suggest your successor, as Chris did in leaving with good grace. When Paul arrived you could see the question in players' faces. 'What will he think about me?'

Paul had an old school mentality about him. To his credit, he gave everybody a chance to bend to his ways and would later acknowledge the quality of the squad he'd been left by Chris. He brought some interesting characters along with him. Kevin Summerfield was his coach. Now Kevin was like a professor of football. He studied the game and knew it inside-out. Everything would be explained down to the last detail.

The other member of the new management team was defensive coach John Blackley. Or 'Sloop' as he was called, right from his days playing with Hibernian. This was derived from the Beach Boys classic *Sloop John B*. Blackley was something of an enemy in our household of Hearts supporters. As a player and a man he was almost a volcano. My dad would always say Blackley was the hardest player he'd ever seen. If he tackled someone then they stayed down. Make no bones about that. John had immense respect from other players and a sort of grudging admiration from opposing fans. They would swear at him and yet all secretly wish he was on their side. John became a big influence on me at Hillsborough, which never stopped him from picking on me for my mistakes.

I got the treatment from Paul Sturrock as well. In training he would often shout across: 'You're just a striker playing at the back!' There was a twinkle in the eye and I think it was partly done for a purpose. If the others could see me getting some stick at 33 then they'd better watch out. The mickey-take was something of a demonstration and I treated it as such. At 18 or 19 I would have taken it to heart but by now it was water off a duck's back.

Under Paul we went undefeated in four games, starting with a 3-0 romp at Wrexham. Then we lost a couple before winning the next four on the bounce. That was the pattern. Two more losses followed and then a three-match winning run at the start of a sequence of 10 games without being beaten. Early in Paul's tenure he appointed a new captain – me. This was after Chris Marsden had decided to quit through injury. Paul called me into his office to give me the news and it was a nice pat on the back from someone I'd grown up admiring so much.

The mickey-taking continued – that was part of Paul's nature – but he'd often come to me for a word. And I found I could go for a chat in his office anytime. There has to be a link between the players and the manager. I was delighted to fill that role. Beyond that, there was a good dynamic between Paul, Kevin and John. You could see they'd been together a long time.

Our approach on the field changed during this time. Paul played more of a percentage style. He understood what was needed at League One level. His philosophy was that defenders in the third tier didn't like being forced to face their own goal. Everything was geared to turning them round through balls played into the channels. In an ideal world this wasn't the way some of us wanted to play. But the proof was in the results. They brooked no argument from anyone, least of all us.

Where he also deserves great credit is that he injected a dash of individual brilliance into the mix. He raided former club Southampton for a young player he'd rated while on the south coast. His name was Kenwyne Jones and he made as big an impact as is possible from any loan player. Jones was just 20 at the time, a big languid striker of pace and skill. Seven goals in as many games from him put us bang on course for the promotion shake-up. We were tenth when he arrived and fourth when he left. Enough said.

Kenwyne scored on his debut in a 4-0 thrashing of Doncaster. There were further single goal contributions in a 3-2 victory over Walsall, a 2-0 win against Port Vale and a 1-1 draw at Luton. Then he bagged a brace against Wrexham (4-0) and was on target again as we saw off Swindon 2-0. But Jones was human after all as he rounded off by failing to score in a 1-1 draw at Bournemouth. And human he was in every sense. Kenwyne, from Trinidad and Tobago, was your typical West Indian. If he'd been any more laid back he'd have been horizontal. I think across the span of those seven games we only saw him seven times in training. He'd wander around in flip-flops complaining about sore toenails or some other ailment. Then he'd turn up and score on the Saturday. Kenwyne was fantastic for us. He turned some of those percentage balls into great passes.

11

Is He Taking the Piss?

Kenwyne Jones' return to Southampton was a big blow but we carried on from the impetus that he had given us. Maintaining a consistent placing of fourth or above, we were well on track for the play-offs. Then a little dip, apparently nothing to worry about at first, threatened to spiral out of control. There seemed scant cause for concern about drawing 1-1 at Colchester in mid-March or being held 2-2 by Torquay at Hillsborough the following week. But this was the start of a seven-match run without a win, including three defeats. You can't choose when you have these blips but the timing in this case was critical.

Going into the eighth game of the sequence at Hull we had slipped to fifth, knowing that if we failed to win at last we could be pipped for a play-off spot. From being in cruise control we'd hit a brick wall. Our visit to the KC Stadium was fraught with danger. On the one hand, Hull were already promoted and had nothing really to play for. But this was to be a party day for them, their players could relax, play their football and enjoy the game. Our mood could not have been in sharper contrast. After working so hard for so long to be in the shake-up, the prize was disappearing before our eyes.

Here's where a manager can once again earn his corn. We

trained as normal the day before the game and then Paul called a team meeting in the canteen at our Middlewood Road training ground. There we all sat waiting for the staff to come in. Then in walked Paul … with a dozen bottles of white wine, a dozen bottles of red and a case of vodka! He plonked the whole lot on the table in front of us and simply said: 'Let's have a drink, lads!'

Now Paul loves his vino but we couldn't believe what we were seeing. 'Is he taking the piss?' What could have been a serious discussion – which was what most of us had expected – turned into a lot of chat and plenty of banter. It wasn't a party exactly because quite a number of the players had cars to drive home but we stayed for one or two. I guess Paul and his staff stayed a lot longer! This was a bit of psychology of course. The gaffer had sensed a feeling of uptightness in the camp and wanted to relax the mood. It worked a treat. We won 2-1 at Hull the next day, though not without some late drama.

I should have got the glory as matchwinner. Did you know that? Maybe you didn't. But no matter, the result was the important thing. We pooped Hull's party by taking a 19th minute lead through Drew Talbot, who was emerging as a promising young forward at that time. Stuart Elliott equalised with a penalty on the hour and we went into the last minute still desperately needing a winning goal to guarantee a play-off place.

We got it right at the end of normal time and James Quinn, the Northern Ireland international who was with us on a short-term contract, is widely credited with scoring the goal. Let me tell you it should have been your versatile striker-turned-defender. I flicked on a long throw and the ball went clean through the keeper's legs and over the line. James followed it into the net to make sure, as every good striker should do. But I know the ball was over and the replay confirms it. Never mind, the goal sparked bedlam among our fans at the away end and James was a great lad, a good signing. It all meant that we were three games away from promotion and two from the magical Millennium Stadium in Cardiff, which was to be the scene of the greatest day of my career.

12

Plain Sailing to Cardiff

Getting to the play-off final is not a prize in itself, even though it might have felt that way at first. We'd still done nothing. Tranmere had finished third, Brentford fourth and we'd squeezed in fifth, a point ahead of Hartlepool. Brentford were the team in our immediate sights with our semi-final opponents having finished just three points in front of us. It looked too close to call – not that it turned out that way – and so Paul Sturrock went for another bout of relaxation therapy. Well, maybe relaxation is the wrong word to describe a canoeing expedition. But it was the sort of distraction we needed from the pressures to come.

The scene was a lake at Rother Valley Country Park on the outskirts of Sheffield. We were all wet-suited up with the players split into teams to race each other. Not Paul Sturrock, Kevin Summerfield and John Blackley, though. They stayed apart from us in the safety of a motor boat. You might form a mental picture of Paul shouting instructions through a megaphone. Except he didn't need that – his mouth was a megaphone. If he and the coaches had taken to a canoe they'd have ended up in the drink, we'd have made sure of that. It's standard practice. As old players, they knew the score and stayed well clear. It was a bit of fun but also bloody hard work.

We were at home to Martin Allen's Brentford in the first leg when ideally, of course, we'd have preferred it to be the other way around. But we didn't give a lot of thought to that. At least we weren't carrying the disappointment of being pipped for automatic promotion and it was a relief just to be in the play-offs. So in that sense the pressure was off us a bit. It's not often you can say that when Sheffield Wednesday are at home in a big match. Certainly, we felt nothing like the pressure we'd been under in winning that end-of-season game at Hull.

The crowd numbered 28,625 on a lovely early summer evening. For atmosphere, in all my time around the club, I'd rate it second only to the win-for-promotion game against Wycombe at the end of the 2011-12 season. Brentford boss Allen was – and still is – a bit of a character and he had them wound up. They were a good side, too, with players such as Stephen Hunt (later of Reading and Wolves), Michael Turner (who progressed to Hull and Sunderland), Jay Tabb (also of Royals fame) and Deon Burton, who went on to join us at Hillsborough. But we played really well. From the first whistle I felt we were comfortable and I never thought we would lose. It was a heck of a strike from Jon-Paul McGovern that gave us a 1-0 lead from that first leg. James Quinn found him with a clever back-heel and JP hit a raking low shot into the bottom corner.

That was as early as the twelfth minute and the place just exploded. We should have got more than the one goal and Brentford were quite happy with the margin.

'The atmosphere was unbelievable,' said Allen afterwards, relieved to be only one goal down. But we were happy with our performance and confident about the second leg in London, despite knowing it would be tough.

Our fans were there in their usual numbers as nearly

11,000 packed into Griffin Park. History shows we came out with a comfortable 3-1 aggregate victory after winning 2-1 in London. But there was a crucial contribution from our goalkeeper David Lucas that should not be lost in the mists of time. It was still 0-0 on the night when David made an incredible save from Burton, who had his back to goal six or seven yards out and caught his shot perfectly on the turn. It came at a good height for a keeper but David showed terrific reactions to turn the ball round the post. We knew the first goal of the night was going to be so, so important. If the Bees had scored then their fans would have been buzzing. Ouch, but it had to be said!

We were in the zone, though. Allen's changing room before the game might have been loud and boisterous but then so was ours. Our ghetto blaster was on full as well. Chances came and went before we managed to give ourselves breathing space. Lee Peacock missed two or three sitters but he put away a header to give us the lead and Chris Brunt doubled it from a free-kick. Brunty hit it as sweet as a nut and a deflection off the wall did the rest. I'll always remember Chris sliding on his knees in celebration in front of our fans. The game was live on Sky and somehow I came away with their man of the match award. I still can't understand why. It was a massive surprise because I thought other players were more deserving. Not that it was much of a prize. It wasn't even a bottle of champagne, just a medal. Still got it, though.

Andy Frampton's late goal for Brentford couldn't take the gloss off our triumph and all roads now led to the Millennium Stadium in Cardiff. I have to be honest here and say we were pleased to be matched with Hartlepool rather than Tranmere whose striker Iain Hume just couldn't stop scoring against us. The semi between those two was something of an epic. Hartlepool won the first leg 2-0 at their place before a reverse of that result at Prenton Park squared it at 2-2 on aggregate. Pools finally went through 6-5 on penalties to set up probably the biggest day in their history.

The same could not be said for us at Wednesday but it was certainly true for many of our players, yours truly included. Even as a veteran I'd never experienced a bigger game, so you can imagine the challenge it presented to so many of our younger players. As I say, it was probably important to sidestep Hume who became a transfer target for us in the weeks that followed only to become a £500,000 signing for Leicester City instead.

Paul Sturrock wanted to keep the build-up to Cardiff as normal as possible. There was no getting fitted up for cup final suits. Paul didn't want any of that lark. He thought it would keep everything more low key if we went down there in our tracksuits. There was no new gear for the lads. We presented ourselves in the same t-shirts we had worn all season. Paul didn't even arrange a visit to the stadium, as so many teams do. We simply turned up in Cardiff the day before the game as we would have done for any away match of that distance. The mood was good on the way down there. Everyone was looking forward to the game and, judging by the demeanour of the lads, I don't think the enormity of the occasion had really sunk in at that point. You always get a few playing computer games on their laptops, some watching videos and others playing cards. But there were plenty of reminders of the emotional extremes that lay ahead of us.

Lincoln City and West Ham players were at the same hotel that bank holiday weekend during which all the play-off finals took place. Lincoln lost their game with Southend ahead of ours and we saw the devastated look on the Imps' players' faces as they came back. Was that going to be us 24 hours on? Later I would have the pleasure of meeting Lincoln's manager, the late Keith Alexander, at an awards evening after I'd played in every position on the field. He was a lovely man. Seeing Keith and his players after a defeat was a reminder of how things could go either way. The media was everywhere but otherwise a quiet evening was had by all. We had a meal and went for a walk. It felt like any other away game at that juncture. Then we watched TV and the cards came out. But most of the lads were in their rooms by 10pm. The nerves didn't really kick in for me until the next day.

That was anything but calm – but for all the right reasons. There was an early sign in the hotel that morning of how different this day was to prove. We were in the foyer when the lift door opened and out stumbled the drunkest man in Cardiff. This was none other than Michael Vaughan, the England cricket captain and a big Wednesdayite. His eyes were like slits and he'd obviously had a good night. Michael staggered through the lobby and out into a taxi bound for the stadium. There were some other supporters in the hotel as well. We had tried to keep the location of the hotel, on the outskirts of the city, a secret but the supporters who tracked us down were all considerate enough to realise we were nervous and to leave us to ourselves.

It was a question of how people would react. There were lads like Brunt and Glenn Whelan who'd come up through academy football. Also Richard Wood and Drew Talbot. The biggest test is always a psychological one. But there was something about that team that gave us an edge and here, for the first time, I have a theory about what made us pull together. The chairman, Dave Allen, had a lot of detractors but very few people know about one of his contributions towards our success that season. He had it inserted in all the contracts that players had to live within fifteen miles of the ground. That applied to the majority of the squad with the ruling having been imposed on all Chris Turner's signings the previous summer; only the loan players were exempt. I would always keep bumping into the other lads after training because there were bunches of us who lived so close together. It's an old fashioned idea really and I doubt any club does it today. Jim McLean used to do it at Dundee United but it's very old school. I'd say there's a lot of merit in the policy.

Although ours was far from the best squad Wednesday had ever had, the team spirit was second to none. It was exceptional. There was never the same camaraderie in my later time with the club. The players might have been better on paper but the bond wasn't as strong. It's something that's very hard to quantify. You can't measure the difference in terms of goals or points. But you can certainly feel it when the atmosphere around a dressing room is right. I know it's become a cliché with every player in the game referring to a 'great set of lads' and trotting out stuff like 'no stars, we all muck in together.' Of course it can't be true everywhere. The problem is knowing when it is really meant. Well, I've been around the block so believe me when I say that the spirit of that team was terrific. It got us through some tight scrapes together. And none was tighter than the one we were to face in Cardiff.

13

Three in a Bed – Wife and Trophy Beside Me!

This is the story of May 29th, 2005 – and quite a bit of the following day! It was only on the coach ride from the hotel into Cardiff city centre that the nerves finally kicked in – for me anyway. At first it was like a ghost town. There were very few people about and you would never have guessed there was a game on of any sort. I suppose the locals simply stayed well clear. Then we turned a corner in the approach to the stadium and the sight in front of us is vividly imprinted on my memory. It's the first unforgettable recollection of a momentous day.

The street was awash with people all bedecked in blue and white. Of course, Hartlepool play in the same colours but our supporters seemed to be everywhere and there was a ripple effect in the crowd as the bus came into view. As word spread along the road you could see people hanging their heads out of pub windows and others sprinting into the road, singing and dancing.

Some ran along with us, banging the side of the bus. And I'll never forget the sight of one guy running next to us for something like half a mile. He had a fag in his mouth and started out with a full pint in his hand, though that didn't stop him jumping up and down, cheering and waving. It was only when we finally reached the stadium that he stopped and went to take a mouthful of beer. But there was nothing left as he'd spilled it all along the way. He threw his glass onto the ground in disgust and the lads pissed themselves laughing.

Moments of light relief like that are priceless in the approach to a big game. Reminders of the size of the occasion were everywhere, including the sight of Chris Waddle, the biggest Wednesday idol of the modern era and an all-time great, being interviewed outside the stadium. It was surreal and I just wish I'd had more eyes in my head to take it all in. The lads had been a bit subdued in the approach to the city but that street scene lifted the mood. Everyone stood up to look around outside. I'm sure spectacles like that help to reduce the tension. Of course, I'm reliving all of this through victorious eyes. The memory bank might have wiped out some of the detail if we'd lost.

We arrived at the ground roughly two hours before kick-off. The bus drives right in under the stadium and from there it's just a walk up some stairs into the changing rooms. We dropped off our bags and wandered out onto the pitch. The stands were empty, of course, and it's then that you can judge the size and majesty of the place. It really is a magnificent stadium. Time for a chat and a chance to take everything in. Maybe a last call to family and friends on the mobile phone before the pre-match team meeting.

Some things you remember and some you don't. I enter a haze when I try to bring back Paul's team talk. No disrespect, but I can't remember a word he said. All I do recall is him saying at some time in the approach to the game that it was the biggest he'd ever been involved with – and that's some statement for a former international who'd been a top player in Scotland. If that was the case, then it certainly applied to all the rest of us. Pre-match routines are different for every player. Mine is nothing extraordinary. I usually get changed straight away while others leave it to the last minute. Then I do a bit of stretching, get some fluid down me and read the match programme. I'm not really one for superstitions either, although until I was made captain I did like to be the last out onto the field for some reason. Steve MacLean was the same in terms of having a little routine. Whenever the referee knocked on the door to call us out, Stevie would always go to the toilet!

By the time we went back onto the pitch for our warm-up the stadium was filling and the noise levels rising. Finally we were back in the tunnel waiting anxiously to emerge into the arena. The place was heaving. Sky TV dictated the timings and I knew there were still the formalities of various introductions and the red carpet line-up. I'd very much reached the point where I just wanted to get on with it. After what seemed like an age, the manager led us from the tunnel followed by myself and our mascot. There were three or four steps up on to the pitch and then came the chance to look around. The one photograph of that day which fills me with most pride is the one capturing that moment. You'll have heard all the clichés about what it's like to walk out for a cup final but let me tell you the feeling is really indescribable. There's this deafening roar, the noise is mind-blowing. I tried to look and find where my family and friends would be sitting – my wife Kerry, my dad, my brother, my mates. Then I was waiting for the moment when 40,000 Owls fans would bellow out our anthem, *Hi Ho Sheffield Wednesday*. In fact, that was a conservative estimate of our support in a crowd of 59,808.

After the ceremonial bit I started to forget about the scene in front of us and concentrate on the game. The time came for the traditional huddle and it was left to me to state the obvious. These are near enough my exact words as I recall them now. 'You don't need me to tell you anything. This is our chance to be legends here. Not many of us will ever get the chance to be involved in something like this again. Let's do it.'

The game lasted 120 minutes and must have been fantastic for the neutral. When I say neutral I'm not referring to those in attendance. I'm really talking about those watching on the box because the crowd in the stadium was fiercely partisan. Our fans caught alight as we made a decent start. We were the better side in the first half and I felt we were dominating play. So I was a bit disappointed we were only 1-0 up at the break, even though it would have been goalless had we not broken through just before the interval. Craig Rocastle played a great one-two with Lee Peacock before pulling the ball back for Jon-Paul McGovern to find the roof of the net from about six yards. It might have looked a simple finish from that distance, in fact, it was anything but. JP did brilliantly to get on the end of that cross and he showed good technique to convert the chance with the outside of his right foot.

I was still a bit uneasy. I knew we were capable of cocking it up. I can say that now with a smile on my face, but we were not immune to the odd error and one mistake would put Hartlepool right back in it. My fears were realised within two minutes of the restart when the equaliser came via a long throw. I jumped to try to clear it but the ball clipped the back of my head and Eifion Williams stole in at the far post to drive home. That wasn't critical from our point of view but the momentum of the match had changed. You could tell that our fans were thinking 'here we go again.'

And it certainly looked that way in the 71st minute when Hartlepool substitute Jon Daly netted a fantastic near-post header from a Gavin Strachan corner.

Time was short and I remember Patrick Collins coming on from the bench. I told Paddy: 'Do not defend. Get forward and go for it. Me and Woody (Richard Wood) will stay back. You just bomb on.'

But it was another of our substitutes, Steve MacLean, on a dramatic comeback from injury, who took centre stage in the drama that turned the game. His 82nd minute penalty equaliser, five minutes after coming on for James Quinn, was a pivotal moment in the club's history. Equally, so was the award itself. Drew Talbot took a tug on his shirt from Chris Westwood and went down. I have to say that when I first saw it I thought it was a soft penalty – and Westwood was sent off into the bargain. But of course we'd have taken it whether we were sure or not. Maybe it was a penalty, though. Having seen it again from another angle, Westwood does have a grip on Drew's shirt which is always a dangerous thing for a defender to do.

Steven had a good record with penalties. He never missed them but he needed balls of steel to take this one. Paul Sturrock on the bench couldn't bear to watch and neither could his captain out on the field. I turned my back to take a peek at it only on the big screen at the other end of the ground. I happened to know Hartlepool's keeper, Dimitrios Konstantopoulos, who'd been third choice at the club I played for in Greece. He's a big lad and fills a lot of the goal. It's a good job Dimitrios went the wrong way because it was probably the worst penalty Stevie's ever taken. He hit it very nervously almost down the middle. But it went in and I think that knocked the stuffing out of Hartlepool.

They had been so close to victory and now the

psychological edge was with us. It was a big demand for them to go into extra-time with ten men and we took full advantage. Our third goal came from a rare mistake by Michael Nelson, a centre half I admired. That said, it took a wonderful strike from Glenn Whelan whose cultured left foot found the corner of the net from the edge of the area. No surprise now, of course, as he's gone on to do that in the Premier League with Stoke.

John Blackley, our defensive coach, had other ideas on the moment that lifted us to promotion. Turning to me afterwards, he said: 'That challenge of yours won us the game.' It was a sliding tackle in the second half of extra-time as we led 3-2. Check a tape of the highlights and you will hear the commentator giving the credit to Richard Wood! But it was my tackle, not that it matters in anything other than that we nipped a moment of danger in the bud.

And so to my most vivid memory of the whole day. It's in my mind in a golden frame. I'll never take that picture down for as long as I live. Time is running down and I'm looking up the pitch. We've cleared the ball upfield and suddenly I notice with surprise that one of their defenders has let it bounce. Drew Talbot, our teenage terrier, has nipped in and headed it past him. He's off and running and I'm standing 30 yards back from the halfway line with an unobstructed view right behind the action.

I'm focusing on Drew but, with the Hartlepool end behind me, I can also see three sides of a stadium packed with Wednesdayites. It's almost slow motion from here. There's a hush but Drew picks up the pace of his run, stepping across the last defender. I see fans start to lift off their seats as Drew homes in on goal. He flicks the ball round the keeper and arms are shooting up into the air. The back of the net bulges and the place erupts. That's it, party started!

The sense of joy and relief engulfed the players and fans simultaneously. But you won't find me in any of the photos of our lads deliriously shaking open the champagne bottles on the pitch. I deliberately took a step back. I wanted to take it all in, to savour the moment.

Looking back, I'm glad I took those few minutes for myself. Otherwise, I wouldn't have remembered half the stuff going on. It was a time for mentally photographing everything, being aware of all the songs being sung. I have to say it was the best feeling ever. Nothing tops it. My freeze-frame of the moment goes back to a piece of advice I was given when I got married in Hong Kong. After the ceremony a pal came up and said: 'Grab your wife and take two minutes to yourselves. Just step away and take in the scene, mentally photograph it.' That's what I did in Cardiff.

Even then, I still notice something I didn't spot at the time whenever I relive the game on video. I haven't done that much lately but YouTube has an edited version of about eight minutes that I like watching from time to time. It still sends shivers down my spine. It was a proud day and one that I will never top whatever I do in the rest of my career. Any time I get annoyed or down I can just put on that video and start laughing as Drew goes through to score that fourth goal. Just brilliant.

The dressing room afterwards was awash with champagne. Everyone was involved from the stats man to the kit man, all hugging and dancing around. Eventually a couple of us tried to find a quiet corner to let it all sink in. Steve MacLean sat down, put a towel over his head and stayed there for about ten minutes, staring at the floor. Paul Heckingbottom and myself went into the training area alongside the changing rooms and slumped against the wall with a few cans of beer between us. We were mentally and physically drained but still feeling the biggest buzz we'd ever experienced. It was such a big thing for us all as individuals as well as the club.

Family members were all given lounge passes, so after I shower I went up there to see my wife, dad and brother. There were eight of my mates who I'd sorted out with tickets for the game. I hadn't been able to get them lounge passes as well but no-one was checking and I sneaked them in. The fact there were players from both sides in the room made it a slightly odd atmosphere. Not only did I know Hartlepool's keeper but I was also acquainted with Ritchie Humphreys, a former Wednesday player. I talked to a few of their guys and got the feeling that, for all their disappointment with the result, they knew it had been a massive achievement just to get to the final.

And so to the team bus for the long ride home. Long is the word. Every player knows how tiresome these journeys can be, especially if you've lost. This one was a lot more bearable, shall we say, although with a party awaiting us back in Sheffield there was still a fair bit of frustration about the hold-ups. Actually, these were to lead to another highlight of the day, as we shall see. Initially, we didn't get far out of Cardiff before crawling along in the enormous volume of traffic leaving the city. Eventually we came to a complete standstill on the motorway. Oh, what the heck – the whole bus was loaded with beer and champagne.

Then all of a sudden the emergency door at the back of the coach was opened. By the time we all looked round, Paul Heckingbottom was off the bus, followed by two or three other lads. Within seconds eight of us were out in the middle of the carriageway – with the trophy – dancing the conga through a line of stationary cars. What a commotion this started! I'd been slumped against a window moments earlier looking at all the bored, frustrated drivers. Suddenly they were all brought back to life by the spectacle in front of them. Many of the cars were filled with our fans. Car horns blared and people were sticking their heads out of windows. Some were even up on the roof of their cars, cheering and singing as we cavorted along with the cup.

Further into the journey we pulled into a service station, knowing there would be a few Wednesday fans there. At first the place seemed almost empty as a line of us players danced into the building, carrying the cup once again. My arms went up in the air with it as we came in sight of everyone. Up went the song: 'Ee aye ee I addio! Up the Football League we go ...'

Everyone around the place seemed to have joined in by the time I reached the balcony at the top of the escalators. 'When we win promotion, this is what we'll sing. We are Wednesday, we are Wednesday, Sturrock is our king!' The whole service station went mental; a completely surreal experience.

In Sheffield we were taken to Napoleon's casino which was owned by the chairman on Ecclesall Road. Initially a celebration had been planned back at Hillsborough but that was vetoed by the police in case the neighbours were nuisanced by fans figuring out where we were and turning up at the stadium. Some of our players never made it out of the casino that night. I had booked rooms for family and friends at the Tankersley Manor Hotel north of the city. It was there, at some time in the morning that I can't recall, that I took to my bed with my wife. And the trophy. It was three in a bed because I wasn't letting it out of my sight.

At breakfast the next day, which I'm amazed I was up in time to eat, I caught a chap looking at me from another table. He looked away and then looked back to see the cup sitting there with us. Suddenly it dawned on him that I was the guy who had lifted it in Cardiff. 'Can I hold it?' he asked, melting into the moment.

14

On a High but Career Up in the Air as Well … Time for a Break

I mentioned all the photographics, mental or otherwise. The one thing you crave when you are on a high is to just freeze the moment. To keep the picture nicely framed and park it on the mantelpiece of your everyday life. You want to carry it with you everywhere for as long as possible. One of the downsides to being a footballer is that the game simply doesn't allow for standing still. Besides, my contract was running down and, regardless of the triumph at the Millennium Stadium, I had no idea whether I would be getting another. Don't forget, I was now 34 years of age.

At any time at any club there are always key decisions to be taken, contracts to be extended, left to roll or even terminated. It's why Sir Alex Ferguson has been so successful; he never stops looking ahead. This is particularly acute at the end of a campaign because there are only three months to the next one and factoring in holidays and the early report back for pre-season training, judgments have to be made straight away. Otherwise there is no time to reshuffle a squad for the challenges ahead. Now throw in two other considerations that made this process all the more urgent in the summer of 2005. The first was that, after going through the play-offs, we were already heading into June, several weeks behind the planning of other clubs. And secondly, of course, we were now in a higher division with all its demands for team strengthening.

Doubtless some sort of start will have been made on this process. It's fair to assume there will have been two strategies prepared in meetings between Paul Sturrock, his chairman and the chief executive. The first scenario, though unwelcome, will have been more straightforward than the second. If Wednesday failed to win promotion, maybe less change would have been needed in the expectation of another challenge. There would also, of course, have been a smaller budget. But if, as proved to be the case, we succeeded then there would be pressure to compete at a higher level and equip the manager with some players who would improve the team.

With the benefit of some new-found journalistic licence, I'm going to award myself a breather at this point. Thought you might like to know how football clubs operate on a day-to-day basis while I continue to wallow in nostalgia. But first let me tie up the loose ends of my uncertainty. I had a couple of days of euphoria after Cardiff and would have been content to let it go on all summer, including the duration of a blissful and well-earned holiday back in Greece.

But it was amazing how quickly the feeling subsided, mainly because I was so unsure of my future. In truth, I would have almost signed on again for nothing. All I really wanted was to play in the Championship and take my career to a new level. Most people would imagine you'd get a jump in wages but I think I signed on pretty similar terms when it was agreed to offer me another year.

I had chats with the chief executive and all I wanted was

the nod that they were keen for me to stay. Paul Sturrock came back to say that he was and that was good enough for me. I probably undersold myself because I just wanted a chance of playing in the second tier. The club knew that as well and played on it. It does make you wonder when boys start coming into the club on three or four times more money but, hey, I was delighted just to be involved.

So what is it that was so seductive about the life that I was involved with? Let me take you through the week of a typical footballer at a typical club. Of course, there are variations to what you are about to read because all managers have differing methods. But in the main – and this is for a week without a midweek game – it goes something like this …

Let's start with the bit people tend to moan about, but then nobody works seven days a week, or should do anyway. I'm talking days off. Not that this applies to my current lifestyle, of which more later! Let me tell you that coaching is a lot harder work than playing. The players normally have Wednesdays and Sundays off – it's that way at the majority of clubs. Most people in the working world get Saturdays and Sundays off. The footballers' weekend is split into two separate days. Certainly, that is the way it was for me at both Dunfermline and Wednesday.

If you're playing in the first team then you report back on Monday for what is a relatively light day, normally a single morning session. For those who think that is a bit soft, it takes your body 48 hours to make a full recovery from intense physical exercise. If you've had an away game at some far-flung place then a lot of your down time will have been swallowed up by the tedium of travel. So Monday's session will usually involve a bit of ball work but nothing too heavy. Training will start at 10am but most players come in around 9 o'clock. It gives them chance to eat a club breakfast, read the papers and chat to team mates with everyone milling around. Then it's down to business on the training pitch.

On certain occasions you'll spend time in the video room if the manager thinks it's necessary to illustrate a few points. That can be at any time of the week. It might be a case of going over certain aspects of our previous game or to highlight some points about our next opponents.

Tuesdays are very different from Mondays. Normally this is the day for a double session. You'll train in the morning, have lunch in the canteen and then get out for more work in the afternoon. More often than not, it's a really physical day. The morning might involve a lot of work with the ball, such as possession games which can become quite intense. Or it could be a case of working on closing down opponents quickly. If anyone is seen not to be doing it effectively then a classic punishment would be to send that player off on a lap of the pitch. In the process, he's also let his side down because they carry on with one less player. The afternoon will typically involve a running session, although not necessarily long distance stuff. It's more about quality than quantity. You'll do a warm-up, then work-out for about 35 or 40 minutes before cooling down. No balls are out.

There was a slight variation to some of this when Paul Sturrock was in charge at Hillsborough. Some morning sessions, like the one on a Tuesday, would involve the squad being split down the middle. Paul believed passionately in the defence working separately under a defensive coach in John Blackley. The midfielders and strikers would work under Kevin Summerfield with Sturrock overseeing the operation and only stepping in when he felt necessary.

Some of the defensive-orientated coaching was incredibly intensive. Us defenders might even be four against eleven!

Other times if we won the ball we'd be required to give it straight back again. There was a lot of emphasis on shape and positioning. This was the first time in my career that I'd experienced this sort of specialist work and John Blackley had a very specific role.

On match days, for instance, all he did was sit in the stand and watch the back four. We might be scoring a brilliant goal at the other end but John would not see it. Even when the ball was with our strikers in the final third, John would be keeping his beady eyes on the back four, making sure that people weren't wandering out of position.

I admired his work and he is very, very good at what he does. Some of the things he would tell me were invaluable. Even as a player of ripe old age, I would find him passing on things that I had never thought of before and I have to say I learned a hell of a lot from John. His input clearly benefited the team as well because, even when we were a point off the bottom of the league at one stage, we still had one of the best defensive records in the division.

The middle of the week would bring our day off. It was during the 2006-07 season that I began to fill that gap by helping to coach the academy youngsters as a bridge towards hopefully a new career. Before that, I would often indulge in the footballer's favourite sport of golf. Or I'd chill out by walking around the shops and grabbing a coffee here or there. It can be difficult being away from the family, especially as the manager would generally frown on me going home in midweek because of the sheer distance between South Yorkshire and Scotland. One of our lads used to journey back to his home in the Midlands and that was more acceptable. So I'd try to make the day as relaxed as possible. I'd got into the café culture during my time in Greece and it was a natural extension of that for me to visit the coffee shops on fashionable Ecclesall Road.

It's back to work on Thursdays, usually for a single session in the morning, and it's nearly always focused on shaping the team ahead of the forthcoming game. There would be the odd week when an afternoon session was added so that a few ideas could be tried out. Fridays would be about working on set-pieces with some fun sessions at the end as the mood became lighter in preparation for the game the next day. We'd have some five-a-side games at Wednesday and split ourselves into teams ... like old boys versus young 'uns ... or England against the rest of the world. The trouble with the latter idea was that our English contingent was never good enough to put up much opposition, especially with Deon Burton claiming to be Jamaican. The rest of the world comprising a few Scots, four or five Irishmen and of course Deon, would rule the roost. The fact that there would be a couple of Scots refereeing didn't harm our cause, either.

Diets have become a hot topic in the modern game. There's no denying that what you eat can affect the way you play. At Wednesday, breakfast and lunch would be provided by the club. I would also get into the habit, of asking the club chef to put something together that John Hills, a player who was living with me at the time, and me could take away for dinner, too.

That way, we were always eating decent stuff. All players are made aware of what they should and shouldn't be eating, but it is very much a personal decision about what you choose to eat. I've known times when nutritionists have come into clubs to give presentations on a proper diet.

At Dunfermline, we even had questionnaires given out and were told to record everything we ate. They wanted to know what we had for breakfast, lunch and dinner every day of the week. But that was ridiculous. Who the hell tells

Three years old … I'm rockin' the grunge look

Primary Two. Bowl cuts were trendy back then!

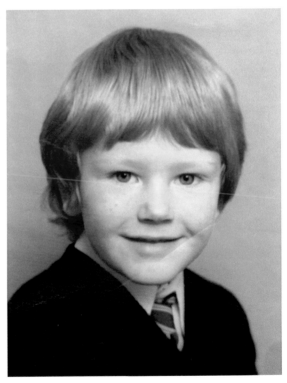

Cornbank Primary class photo. If you can't spot me, look for the
red hair – I'm second from the left on the middle row

Not quite Cardiff
... BB Select XI

Penicuik High School first year ... Champions!

Eskmills BC. My dad is front right and Alex Young, front left

Hutchison Vale Colts 1988

Lee with his bottle of Whyte & Mackay whisky

✔ PLAYER OF THE WEEK

Lee in the limelight

WHITBURN'S goal-den boy, Lee Bullen, collected this week's Whyte & Mackay/Pink Player-of-the-Week prize and admitted that he now had to prove himself all over again.

The 21-year-old striker, who was the Pink's player of the season last year, collected his bottle of Whyte & Mackay for his performance in last week's 1-1 draw with Blackburn.

But, within two hours of being told of his success, his prize-winning performance was soon forgotten as Whitburn slumped to a 5-2 defeat at Livingston.

He said: "Of course, I'm very happy to accept the award, especially so soon after winning a magnum of champagne from the Pink, but losing so badly in midweek has taken the shine off it.

WHYTE & MACKAY
SCOTCH WHISKY

"I scored a couple of penalties, but I feel I now have to prove myself again."

And he admitted that the recognition had come as a big surprise. "I didn't even feel that I played all that well against Blackburn - it must have been the goal which stood out."

The former Meadowbank and Stenhousemuir striker controlled a cross and chested it down into the path of Keith Ferguson, who blasted home a half- volley from 20 yards. "It was a great goal, but I need to score a few more myself," said Lee.

Good times at Whitburn Juniors

With Mike Duxbury and his boys in Hong Kong

Trouble! My brothers Gary and Glyn

Best men in 'skirts'

Hong Kong League XI with Big Jack

Hong Kong FA Cup Final 1995-96. Golden v South China

Golden XI v England –
before the Dentist's chair!

My debut for Kalamata
v OFI Crete

Derby day v Pyrgos and my second match

GOAL! Not a bad way to start against our biggest rivals

Promotion with Kalamata in the 1998-99 season

Kalamata 1999

With Greek
international Thanasis
Kostoulos, my
Kalamata teammate

Always good to score
– even as a sub

Bitter sweet memories. The Scottish Cup Final against Celtic

A sad farewell to Dunfermline after the final

May 17th 2005, the greatest day of my playing career

It's sinking in!

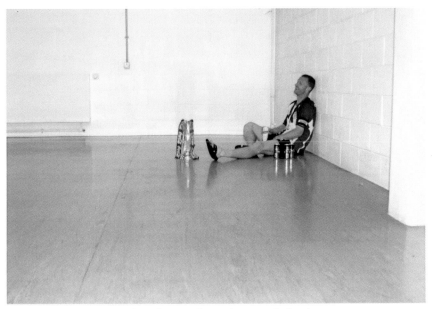

The aftermath … deserved that!

'Scotland, Scotland's number one'

Clearing from defence against Wolves

Welcome to the coaching side. Falkirk FC

With my two wonderful kids, Jodie and Jay

Good tan! Defensive advice for the Sheffield Wednesday Academy players

Pre-season 2013-14. Football in the sunshine

the truth on forms like that, anyway? I know players who live on pizzas and takeaways most of the time. For myself, I didn't completely abstain – I love a good cheeseburger – but I knew the limits. If I went out for a meal at some point during the week I would always be mindful of what I was eating. I wouldn't stick to the rules 100% but would try to eat the right things at the right time. For instance, if you like red meats then it's better to go for them early in the week. Later, it's more beneficial to have pasta and high-carb meals.

In previous years, footballers have been associated with a massive drinking culture. Still are to some extent. It's a hard link to shake off. But those incidents are exceptional rather than typical these days. Besides, while there is merely advice about diet, there are strict rules on alcohol. Every club has them and they are rigidly enforced. Players know they shouldn't be out drinking for at least 48 hours before a game. If they are caught out boozing on a Thursday or Friday night then they will be fined. Even being caught drinking on a Wednesday night wouldn't make a manager too happy, so that's why Tuesday became a popular night out on midweeks without a game.

It would be acceptable then and frankly, it would be stupid to chance your arm later in the week. If you go out for a drink – anywhere at any time – the chances are that your club will find out. There's a constant stream of messages about where players have been spotted and what they've been up to. There's no hiding place, even if you're not doing anything wrong. In fact, I very rarely went out in Sheffield, especially after a defeat. The only time I ever went out after a defeat, and it was a game where my mistake had cost us, I had a horrible night, my worst in Sheffield.

One occasion comes to mind when the first team were

away in midweek and there were six or seven injured boys who didn't make the trip. Richard Wood and Paul Heckingbottom were among them. They decided to go out together to cheer themselves up a bit. It was as innocent and harmless as that. The amount of texts and emails the club received slaughtering those players was absolutely unbelievable. There were comments questioning how they could be injured and what they were doing out drinking if they weren't fit. In reply, it has to be said that some fans just don't realise the mental torture of being out injured. All you want to do is play. Instead you have to sit there watching five-a-side games and seeing the other boys get ready for Saturday. No-one wants to be sitting on the sidelines and sometimes you need a bit of a lift to get through it.

There is an element to the game now where it seems like supporters are allowed to do or say whatever they like to a player and the player has the responsibility to just take it on the chin without responding. It's as if it has become the fans' prerogative to hurl abuse, chant obscenities and bring things to an entirely personal level while the player is charged with doing nothing by way of his duty as a role model. It takes a lot of patience at times and things have got out of kilter in this regard. I suppose supporters probably haven't changed that much. Footballers are more in the public eye now and the game has a higher profile than ever before.

I'm fortunate in that I never had supporters approaching me in public to criticise me. Don't get me wrong, there might have been a few standing on the other side of the bar slagging me off to their mates, but my interaction with fans has been positive.

Most of them – probably 99% – are incredibly supportive. Most simply want to get you to sign an autograph or take a photo of you with their phone. Some players see this as an intrusion but I've always appreciated it. Besides, it's always nice to get a pat on the back from people. I think it can be more of an intrusion for members of your family, though.

That was one fortunate side to having Kerry up in Scotland while I was playing down in Sheffield. It meant she didn't suffer any invasion of privacy. In Greece, it was a lot different. We might be out for a meal together when some stranger would come over, pull up a chair and start talking. In Greece, more than here, Kerry was far likelier to be completely ignored in that situation despite being sat opposite me at the table. Perhaps there's a more chauvinistic nature in the culture. Blokes would sit and talk straight at me without even acknowledging Kerry, which isn't nice. Very frustrating, but part of the job, I suppose.

15

Being Scottish, Ginger-Haired and in Goal – at Millwall!

In some ways, season 2005-06 was a bit of a write-off for me – but one aspect of it has been truly written-up. I did something that created a bit of history. And maybe it'll stay in the history books for all time. Has any player previously played in every position on the park in the course of one season? The answer is no as far as I'm aware. Will it be done again? Unlikely, I would have thought. But then so many strange things happen in this great game of football that you can never be entirely sure of anything.

For starters, I wasn't even certain that I'd still be at the club after winning promotion to the Championship. Then there was the question of winning a place in Paul Sturrock's side. Well, I did that all right – but in another sense I didn't. Not one place, I mean. Had I done so, this section of the book wouldn't exist. There is always a bright side, a positive from a negative.

Don't forget that prior to coming home to Dunfermline from my global travels I'd never played regularly anywhere other than in attacking positions. It was either up front or out wide on either flank. All of a sudden I was playing everywhere – in the space of one year! Let's just say I wasn't exactly thrilled about it at the time. Not to start with, anyway. I was in and out of the side, filling in here and filling in there. It's difficult being a professional footballer if you're not given the chance to play.

There was a spell when I was basically being paid to be a PR man, turning up at events, shaking hands and giving away tickets. That's part of being captain anyway and I didn't mind doing a lot more of it because I had the spare time with my family being up in Scotland. I would volunteer for a lot of it. But underneath it all, the only thing you really want to do is to play.

Naturally enough, Paul Sturrock had strengthened the side. Among the acquisitions were a couple of defenders, Madjid Bougherra and Graham Coughlan, both centre backs who would make it hard for me to get a place there. With Richard Wood also at the club and progressing well, it turned out that I never got a run in any one position. Not that I had any hard feelings about that because it was the manager's job to improve the squad. Being considered versatile is a handicap in one respect and an asset in another. Had I not been adaptable I would have sat on my backside for most of that first season back in the Championship. Instead, I became what used to be referred to as a utility player. Necessity is the mother of invention … that's another apt saying. But let me give you another one that best describes my status around that time – jack of all trades and master of none. The manager knew he could stick me here and there, and while I would not give a nine-out-of-ten performance I could usually manage a six or a seven.

It was like being the ball on the inside of a pinball machine. Here is an example of one typical spell in my time at Wednesday. I played at right back and then got switched to the left when Paul Heckingbottom was injured. After a couple of games there I was at centre defence to replace Graeme Lee. From being on the right side of the centre back pairing alongside Guy Branston I was switched to the left when Guy was suspended after being sent off at Tranmere. Suddenly I had played in every position across the back four within half-a-dozen games. Then there were the times when I came on in central midfield against Millwall and Leicester. In fact, I had a few reserve games in that position and thought I did okay, but it never went further. If the gaffer ever really thought about me playing there properly, he certainly never gave me a fair crack of the whip. I became the ultimate utility man, though I think it worked against me as well. I was a good body to have on the bench. It was from there that I eventually played everywhere, up front, on the wing, you name it. And it's a wonder I wasn't also on the turnstiles when the fans came to our games!

Mind you, I did play from the start on the day that is best remembered from that season. It was at the New Den, the notoriously inhospitable home of Millwall, on February 4th, 2006. I was called up at right back in a defence shorn of the injured Graham Coughlan. Both clubs were down near the bottom battling against the drop and Paul Sturrock decided this was a game we had to win. To that end, he took a bit of a gamble. He went in with no goalkeeper on the bench because Paul wanted an extra striker among the substitutes. He'd done it before a few weeks earlier. Nicky Weaver was in goal on that occasion and it turned out that he went down under a heavy challenge. I was on the bench at the time and started warming up. It was a bit tongue-in-cheek but I told the gaffer I'd be happy to go in goal. In the event, Nicky got up and we got out of jail.

And so to Millwall. All was well until just before half-time when our keeper, David Lucas, went up for a simple cross. He dealt with it easily but landed awkwardly on his knee and jarred it badly. Paul must have been thinking that all his plans had gone up in smoke as it became obvious that David couldn't continue. It was one of those situations where everybody looks at each other, wondering what to do.

Glenn Whelan was willing to go in goal and so was Deon Burton. The two of them were discussing it near the touchline. Someone needed to take responsibility. I reasoned that we couldn't afford to lose Glenn from the centre of the park, plus there was a ready-made replacement for me on the bench in Drissa Diallo. Added to which, I was the tallest and willing to do the job. As captain, I felt it should be me and so I went to the gaffer with my offer to go in goal. I remember he gave me a hard stare. It must have been for a couple of seconds, looking right into my eyeballs. Then he gave me the nod. It's a bit like somebody stepping up to take a penalty. You can tell by looking at them whether they are nervous or not, whether they are in the right frame of mind. I had no fear at the time. Not that it was any sort of preparation, but I'd been in the nets once before in an Under-15s game for Dunfermline when our keeper failed to turn up. I think we lost that game, though!

I suppose Paul reasoned that, apart from saying 'I'll do it,' I at least had the right physique for the job. Whether I could catch a ball or save a shot was another matter, of course. Nobody could know the answer to that, not even me. What I did know is that I had grown a pretty thick skin by that stage of my career. But it still turned out I had to grow a few extra layers that day. Playing in Scotland, I was used to hostile crowds. Let me tell you that, by any standards, Millwall is something else for an opposition player. It's not called the Lion's Den for nothing and you can imagine the treatment I got when I stepped between those posts. Well, perhaps you can't. You had to be there and you had to be me.

The Millwall fans were right behind me when I took over from David, ours being at the other end of the ground. I was just glad it was nearing the end of the half. Mind you, they didn't waste their opportunity. Most of the stuff hurled at me was unprintable. It was 'you Scottish this' and 'you ginger that.'

Just as well, perhaps, that I didn't understand some of it because of the east London accents. But there was no mistaking it for the non-stop abuse that it was. Don't get me wrong. With it being a tight ground and such a volatile crowd, Millwall is a fantastic place to play. I didn't let it get to me. In fact, I turned round and smiled at those fans. They were playing the pressure game, naturally doing anything they could to put me off. As such, it was a psychological test. Not that I wasn't glad to see out the half at 0-0 and get down the other end where our supporters were waiting.

At the break, the manager was very honest with us and with himself. He came in and said: 'Look lads, I've left you up shit creek here, but if you go out and get a win or a draw then you're heroes.'

I was a little nervous at first, but once you've caught the ball to settle yourself down it's more a case of getting your positional sense right. In training, you usually find that, given the choice of playing anywhere, all the strikers want to go in goal and all the keepers want to play up front. A few of us had done the job before as a muck-around at the end of training, though never more seriously than that. In fairness, the manager didn't really like it. Only occasionally at Sheffield Wednesday would we play a five-a-side where everyone could play where they wanted. In Greece we would do it all the time.

It was nice to come out for the second half at the New Den in front of our fans and, in fact, I came out early. Clearly, I needed to have a work-out so Billy Mercer, our goalkeeping coach, joined me on the pitch. It was about getting a feel for the ball, quite literally. Cries of 'Scotland's number one' from our supporters helped break the tension.

I'd had nothing of great importance to do up to the interval but I knew that the second half would be different. Millwall's manager was bound to have had a right go at his players telling them to put me under pressure from the word go. The message will have been to get everything in on the goalkeeper, balls and bodies, long throws, free-kicks, corners, everything. Most managers would demand exactly the same in that situation.

Around the hour mark, with the game still goalless, Millwall had a free-kick on the edge of our box. The shot came in and it was heading for the top corner. I had to dive high to the left and managed to touch the ball with my right hand across my body. The fingertip was just enough to take the ball safely behind the goal via the crossbar.

Cue an inswinging corner from David Livermore. As it came into the six yard box I went up to punch it along with their striker Peter Thorne and a couple of our defenders. I got knocked over as we all went for the same ball. Somehow all of us managed to miss it and it ended up in the back of our net direct from Livermore's corner. There was a mass celebration away to the side of my end as Millwall players raced to rejoice with their supporters.

Unbeknown to them, I went up to complain to the referee, Steve Tanner, saying, 'Surely we should have a free-kick for a foul.' I thought my hand was being held back from making contact with the intended punch. There were so many bodies around me and I was just watching the ball, trying to get something on it. I had players in front of me pushing me back and players pushing from the side as well, so you are automatically claiming a foul of some kind.

I though the referee had given the goal as he pointed towards the centre circle with his right arm. But then, as we all surrounded him, he pointed his left hand down to the ground. Luckily enough, he gave us that free-kick, and it certainly was lucky as I shall explain later.

There were still about eight Millwall players in blissful ignorance of the decision. They were carrying on their celebration as I put the ball down to take the free-kick. The linesman didn't help the home players at all because I don't think he was sure what was happening. But he must have seen us play on and he should really have given them the nod. Chris Brunt and Glenn Whelan shouted to me to get the ball down quickly and play on. I rolled it out to Chris and he went on the counter-attack. Brunty ran sixty yards with it as the rest of our lads stormed upfield.

Still it hadn't clicked with some of the Millwall boys but suddenly they woke up to what was happening and sprinted back but too late. The ball dropped to right back Frankie Simek who somehow scored with the crappiest volley you've ever seen. Their keeper made a bit of a horror show. The ball must have bounced about six times before entering the net. But no matter, we were one-up in a vital game and, what's more, we held on to the three points.

Frankie had a nose bleed every time he went over the halfway line. I don't know what was more surprising about that day – me keeping a clean sheet or him scoring. Such were the odds against either event that we might have beaten any team in the world that day!

The Millwall players were too stunned even to hound the

referee. They just sank to their knees in disbelief. The whole thing was bizarre. From thinking they were one-up, they were one-down in the blink of an eye. The Millwall lads were too shell-shocked to respond, as the rest of the game proved. I was standing back in my goal and so I didn't get to take part in the celebratory scrum, but I did turn around to the Wednesday fans behind my net and gave them a big two-fisted salute. Of course, you'd be 100% gutted about it if the boot was on the other foot but the Owls had seen enough bad luck and we deserved that rub of the green.

We held on to Frankie's 63rd minute goal and the atmosphere in the dressing room afterwards was one of disbelief. 'How the hell did we keep a clean sheet with you in goal?' was the standard response. But let me introduce you to the real heroes of the day. They were our centre backs, Richard Wood and Drissa Diallo. They were just unbelievable. They kicked everything, headed everything. Magnificent, immense. The other hero was Steve Tanner. He had to be the bravest referee in Britain to disallow that goal. It took real courage to take a decision like that in front of those fans.

And yet I think he got it wrong!

Having watched the whole incident again on YouTube, I have to admit that I genuinely think it was one of my own defenders, either Richard or Drissa, who knocked me out of the way. I mentioned this at a Football League presentation at the end of that season where I received an award for playing in every position. There was some acknowledgment of my honesty, which I appreciated. I got away with a few things that day.

Although I had to dive among a few feet and tipped one round the post from thirty yards, there were no point-blank saves. It all felt pretty routine. But it was still a proud moment for me because of the pressure of the game. And it'll make a good quiz question one day. Talking to some supporters it's their biggest memory of me, ranking even above lifting the promotion trophy in Cardiff.

The only let-down was that I didn't keep my place – in goal, at least. I got dropped! Ha ha. Paul Sturrock pulled me and said I wouldn't be in goal. What an absolute disgrace! But I did at least stay in the side and, funnily enough, I found myself on the left side of midfield. Taking corners as well!

We had a lot of injuries that season and eventually limped to safety, thanks to a few notable victories including a 3-1 win at Wolves. One big disappointment was that Sheffield United did the double over us, winning 1-0 at Bramall Lane and then 2-1 at Hillsborough. That second defeat was clinched by a mistake from yours truly, though the goal that resulted came from one of the best finishes I've ever seen. I failed to cut out a cross which found Ade Akinbiyi. Not that I worried too much at the time as he was outside the area. Ade was a nightmare to play against because of his physical strength but a lot of people would agree that finishing was not his strongest suit. On this occasion he rifled the ball from one side of the 18 yard box right into the far corner. It was a fantastic strike and, although we came back towards the end, I have to admit United deserved to win.

Glad to say I started all the last seven games, having been recalled for our big win at Molineux. We were unbeaten in our final four matches. A vital home victory over Norwich was followed by a win at Brighton, a Hillsborough draw with Reading and a last-day triumph at Derby. So we ended a very difficult season in what, from the point of view of many observers, would have been surprisingly good shape.

16

What a Send-Off!

Taking stock for a moment, I'd come to Hillsborough for one year initially and had now completed two. And I would go on to double that to four before the old warhorse finally departed. Not too bad for a bloke who entered his third season at the club as a 35-year-old. This would be a season of upheaval on and off the field. We had a change of management which always brings a challenge to even the most established players. Happily, we ended the 2006-07 campaign in buoyant fashion to leave yours truly stargazing further into the future. But the way I began the season is probably best forgotten.

Well, it would be forgotten but for the fact that writing this book obliges me to mention it. The record shows that I was sent off at Preston in our first game of the season. It was a straight red for a challenge on Matt Hill in the 57th minute. I owe the other lads because we still went on to get a point from a goalless draw that day.

In fact, it was the first time I had ever been sent off. And me, an ugly brute of a 35-year-old defender. Don't ask me how that's possible but it's true. Other than Preston, I don't think I've been sent off at any level, schoolboys upwards. Some might think it's nothing to be proud of, especially for someone who was now getting paid for making challenges rather than riding them as I did in my days as a striker. But let's not forget that my biggest trait was my committed approach rather than my technical ability. So I must have been committed in quite a cultured way. I'm more than happy with the fact that this was my one and only red card. I must have timed most of my tackles pretty well.

What I'm not happy about is that even this one single red card should never have been on my record. At Deepdale I was going for the ball and not the man. I genuinely thought I nicked it. Okay, the boy went up in the air a few feet but he wasn't injured. I felt hard done by. I just told the referee words to the effect of: 'You're wrong.' I did so with my Scottish twang and he probably couldn't make out the swear words!

When I returned to the side after a standard three-match ban it was for a home League Cup tie with Wrexham that we managed to lose 4-1. I got booked in that as well ... and again in the next league game, a big Yorkshire derby with Leeds that saw us edged out 1-0 at Hillsborough.

Most of the games seemed to be tight but we just couldn't seem to win. There followed a 0-0 draw at Southend, a 1-1 at home to Stoke and then 2-1 defeats to Hull and Derby. Considering we then lost 1-0 at Sunderland, making it six matches without a win to add to the solitary early triumph at Sturrock's former club Plymouth, there was a bit of tension building.

Chris Brunt took the edge off with a brilliant last minute volley that saw us beat Barnsley 2-1 at Hillsborough on October 14th. But four days later we crashed 4-0 at Colchester and Paul was sacked. It was at the old Layer Road ground but wherever it was played it was destined to be one of those nights when nothing went right for us. The reverse was true for the opposition. Everything Colchester hit went in. They were all great goals. For instance, Greg Halford zipped one in from an angle some 35 yards out.

The players had no inkling of the pressure Paul was under. Everyone was surprised when he moved on the next day. It was sad. We understand what he'd gone through to get the team promoted and keep us at the new level. He was both liked and respected in the dressing room, which is not always a common combination. There are managers you like but can't respect and those you respect but can't like. For me, Paul ticked both boxes. He was always up front with you. Yes, he could say some cutting things at times. But you always knew there would be nothing said by him behind your back. There is too much of that in football generally. It was always to your face with Paul. That said, players are as aware as managers that football is a results-based business.

Paul had also been immensely popular with our supporters. They were even more stunned by his departure and that stirred up the atmosphere for our next match at home to Queens Park Rangers. But it's amazing how players can switch off to that type of thing. I wasn't playing that day and people have remarked that it must have been strange for those who were. The pre-match demonstrations against chairman Dave Allen and his board spilled over into the game. In fact, I've heard it said that they lasted right through the 90 minutes. But the lads just blanked everything out. How did I not notice? Maybe I was just too engrossed in the game to bother with anything else. To everyone's credit we won 3-2 in an incredible ebbing and flowing game that could have gone either way but ended up in our favour.

For Sean McAuley, stepping up from academy manager, it was the start of a fantastic spell in caretaker charge. The place needed stabilising and he was very calm about it, trusting the players and letting us manage things for ourselves. We drew 2-2 at Wolves before I returned to the action in another home cliff-hanger which turned into a 3-2 victory over Crystal Palace. We were trailing 1-0 and 2-1 at various stages. I came on for Graham Coughlan in the 86th minute and Steve Maclean scored our winner in injury time. Then came another home success, 2-1 over Leicester, and a 2-0 victory at Ipswich. I was now established at centre-back again alongside Madjid Bougherra.

Sean's record as caretaker read: Played 4 Won 3 Drawn 1. In the modern game, that sort of run has normally been more than sufficient to secure a temporary manager the job on a full-scale basis. But Dave Allen was a strong character. Having withstood the massive protest over the Sturrock dismissal, he was determined to do what he thought was right for the club. Sean had an important position in developing young players and Dave clearly felt recruiting an experienced manager was better for Wednesday in the longer term. As it turned out, the chairman could do no wrong because his choice of Brian Laws produced a continuation of the revival which Sean had provided in further wins over Crystal Palace and Leicester. Brian's first game delivered a 2-0 victory at Ipswich before the minor hiccup of a 3-1 defeat at Coventry. We went unbeaten in the next four, winning three of them including a great 4-1 victory at Leicester. Brian and his assistant, Russ Wilcox, had been picked out by the chairman after their Scunthorpe team had given us a tough time. It was a great opportunity for the pair of them.

Then came another temporary upturning of the applecart. Our keeper, Mark Crossley, had an unbelievable spell of fortune, both bad and good, just before Christmas. First, he was injured at home to Birmingham – and guess who went between the posts in our 3-0 defeat? We were 2-0 down anyway but I was determined to extend my clean sheet from the Millwall game. I was gutted to lose a goal right at the end. Marcus Tudgay played a terrible back pass which left Cameron Jerome one-on-one with me. I never got near it.

Fast upon this came an amazing 3-3 draw at home to Southampton. The last goal of the six, right at the end, was scored by ... Mark Crossley. He came up for a corner and got us a point with a fantastic header. Mark's a big unit, unstoppable when he gets moving with the ball in his sights. But I'd have been proud of the contact he made on that ball.

Boxing Day 2006 was almost literally a boxing day as I went into a tough duel with Stoke's 6' 4" striker Mamady Sidibe. This was another stand-out game as we won 2-1 at the Britannia Stadium. I gave them their goal with a typical Bully error – a back pass that fell short. Marcus, it's not only you! Sidibe cashed in. Hell, he and Ricardo Fuller were tough, tough characters and took some holding. Stoke still have that physical, direct element to their game. Thankfully on this day we played the ball around really well, passed them off the park in fact.

That hard-fought win at Stoke was followed by what was billed as another toughie, away to our neighbours from Barnsley. But we came out 3-0 winners at Oakwell and suddenly, after seemingly facing a fight against relegation in the run-up to Paul's sacking, all the talk was about getting into the play-offs. This was the peak of my career in that sense. I was so close at that point to a fairytale finale in the Premier League ... if they kept me on, of course.

It certainly didn't harm my prospects that I came in for some high praise from the Sky commentary team during an FA Cup third round replay at Manchester City. We lost 2-1 in the end but the highlight for me was my equaliser.

This was at the new City of Manchester Stadium – now the Etihad – and we turned up in our bus in the underground car park while City players drove up in flash cars and threw their keys to valets who parked them. So we saw how the other half live yet still gave them a run for their money. I'll never forget my goal, even though most of the credit belongs to Chris Brunt for a typically deadly set-piece delivery. I got away from Micah Richards and in front of everybody to flash a header into the net. Nicky Weaver in City's goal (later to join us at Hillsborough) is still grasping fresh air as we speak! Considering the opposition, it was as good a single moment from a purely selfish point of view as I've had in the game.

Something else I won't forget is playing as the team's only recognised defender for the entire second half of a home game against Sunderland. Graham Coughlan and myself had the company of two midfielders in the full-back positions because of an injury crisis at the club. It was so bad that there weren't even any defenders on the bench and so when Graham was forced off late in the first half, it was me against the world! Despite that, we pulled back from 0-3 to 2-3, only for a late goal to secure Sunderland's 4-2 win.

The team needed steadying after a rocky spell and I was glad to have Steve Watson, signed on loan from West Bromwich, alongside me. Our 3-2 win over Leeds in the Elland Road derby of March 3rd 2007 stands out for one of the best goals I've ever seen. Chris Brunt won the ball on the left hand touchline some 40 yards from goal. Most players would have just taken it down the line. Not Brunty. He looked up, saw the Leeds keeper off his line, and instantly unfurled an exquisite chip to land the ball in the net. 'World class' was commentator Clive Tyldesley's description. We all stood looking on open-mouthed. It was unbelievable awareness and technique. Had it been Beckham in the Premier League we would still have been watching it time after time.

Mind you, my 'goal' that day was even better. Take off the quotation marks. It was a goal and a stunning one at that. Only at the wrong end! We were 3-0 up and I must have thought the game was too easy. Maybe it needed something to keep our fans on their toes. Whatever, I provided it. The ball was six yards outside our box and I took this sideswipe off balance to clear it. From that distance I somehow sliced it into my own net. You could say it was a great finish and I wouldn't be able to do it again if I tried for the rest of my life. But it certainly didn't deserve to eclipse some great goals that day. Apart from Chris's effort, Marcus Tudgay's and Jermaine Johnson's were both wonderful strikes.

This was part of a terrific spell for the team that made the top six a distinct possibility. Successive wins over Crystal Palace, Cardiff, Ipswich, West Brom and Coventry stretched our unbeaten run to 10 games. Then came a 2-0 defeat at Birmingham that ended our hopes. What a chance for us as they had a man sent off. Things can turn on small things. Kenny Lunt hit the bar just seconds before Birmingham broke away and scored their first goal. But it had been a thrilling season of great progress considering our toil of the previous campaign and our struggling start.

17

And Another False Start ...

Season 2007-08 proves to be my last at Sheffield Wednesday. But who'd have thought I'd make it this far? Four years? I'd have more than settled for that when I first came south. Now I was approaching another crossroads in my career, but also, more importantly, in my whole life. As one who has always protected his family and shielded them from the nastier side of the football spotlight, it's painful for me to put my marital break-up on the record in print. But I feel it is necessary to do so at this point and I shall express myself as honestly as possible, with due regard to the feelings of those involved. There is no blame attached to them anyway as the blame is all mine.

I'm also never one to make excuses and there is no way I'm going to look for any to explain away my shambolic start to my final season with the Owls. Yet it is a fact that I was chasing my tail on and off the field in this period. Beside the worry over my domestic circumstances, I was also taking a university degree and if that wasn't enough, sitting a major coaching licence at the same time. On reflection, I don't know how I managed it all, what with all the trips back to see my young kids in Scotland.

Anyway, none of this explains the absolute shocker I had at Ipswich on the opening day of the campaign. Why is it that

I kept having these nightmare starts? It was a lovely August day in Suffolk and we were all up for it. We end up losing 4-1 but that's not even half the story where I'm concerned. Well, perhaps it is in a literal sense because I played only half the match. Then I did something afterwards that was so shameful and uncharacteristic that I really can't explain it.

A year earlier I was sent off on the opening day. This time I conceded a penalty in the first minute. Ipswich scored, of course, and I was hauled off at half-time. If I'd been manager I'd have done the same. I was absolutely raging with myself over my performance. I don't think I've ever been so personally disappointed.

After the game, I didn't wait for the other players to troop in. I just went and sat by myself on the bus. As manager, Brian Laws asked where I was but said nothing to me on the long, wretched journey back to South Yorkshire. On the Monday morning though, he pulled me in and had a go at me. Quite rightly so. My behaviour was unprofessional. I was in the wrong. As captain, I should I have been in that dressing room with the lads. Brian must have been steaming in the bus. I suppose things could have flared up if he'd said something at the time. Every manager has his own way of dealing with these things. I was dropped for the next game – again, quite rightly – and all I can say is that the incident was totally out of character. Never before or since have I behaved that way.

It's funny – or maybe not! – how starting the season on the wrong foot can cost a team far more than just the three points dropped on the day. That Ipswich defeat, and more importantly the performance, seemed to set the whole tone for what followed.

In short, we lost ALL the first SIX matches. This, remember, was a side hoping to follow up on a near miss on the play-offs. That said, we had lost some of our best players in the summer. Chris Brunt went to West Brom for £3m, Madjid Bougherra (Charlton £2.5m) and Steve MacLean (out of contract, to Cardiff).

Although Franny Jeffers arrived as a high profile capture, there was a struggle for the manager to replace what he lost and it took two emergency signings to pull our season round. Graham Kavanagh and Michael Johnson, two very experienced players, stiffened the side for a home game with Hull which we won 1-0 courtesy of a rare goal from Franny. What a pity that injuries wrecked his time with the club because this goal was an absolute gem. He cut in from outside the box and bent the ball into the top corner, easily the highlight of his time at Hillsborough. Gradually the pressure eased on the team and the manager from that point. Amazing to think, by the way, that Hull went on to win promotion to the Premier League under Phil Brown that season.

For me – and most of us, I imagine – the high point of the season was beating Sheffield United 2-0 at our place in January. I mentioned how the Blades deserved to defeat us in the Hillsborough meeting of two years earlier (before their year in the Premiership). Well, this time our victory was thoroughly well merited. Nothing will beat the experience at Cardiff, of course, but for atmosphere this came close. This was payback time for us and I'll always remember an early moment in the game. Talking, as we were just now about setting the tone, this was another example of how that can be done within the context of 90 minutes.

As right back I was up against a young lad called Lee Martin who was on loan at Bramall Lane from Manchester United. He was quick and clever and I knew he could give me a very hard time if he got his confidence up. Well, I never let him. I won a great tackle on Martin in the first minute. I knew I could have got booked if I was out with the execution, but I timed it just right and won the ball fair and square. My confidence soared and his dipped. It's a great feeling when you know you are getting the better of your opponent. You can look into his eyes with an expression that says: 'I've got you.' I felt I could run all day. So did we all. Akpo Sodje and Marcus Tudgay scored the goals to see us home. In the return game at Bramall Lane in April we very nearly did the double, going two-up only for United to level it at 2-2. But Wednesday were only to be denied the dream double for a further year. Unfortunately, I had moved on by then but I'm glad, at least, that I sampled the special feel of these games and knew how good it felt to win.

January '08 was bitter sweet because it was at the end of that month that I was told my contract would not be renewed. I was surprised but only a little. After all, I wasn't getting any younger – coming up 37 at this point. Where the manager was concerned, you couldn't really say we were best buddies but there was a feeling of mutual respect between us. By coming to tell me his decision as early as he did, Brian Laws gave me the opportunity and time to find a new club. I certainly respect him for that. Some managers wouldn't do that and would just leave you in the dark. I was still captain and there was no point walking around with my bottom lip out. There was a still a responsibility for me to lead by example. Besides, the first team is a far better shop window than the reserves – another reason for keeping your attitude spot-on. It's also why I'm still so disappointed with myself over the Ipswich debacle.

I accepted Brian's decision and did my best. But it wasn't about me anyway. The last thing I wanted was to leave the club relegated and back in League One. It would have wiped out so much of what we achieved at the Millennium Stadium and taken some of the shine off a great memory. I took it as my mission to ensure we stayed in the Championship, whether I was in the team or supporting the lads by my presence in the dressing room. There was a particularly crucial game at Leicester who were among our rivals at the bottom end of the table.

Leon Clarke produced a fantastic lob to finish things off at 3-1 in our favour. I played that day but only for half the game after one of those calculated fitness gambles. I'd been suffering with a hamstring injury and knew it could go at any time. So did the manager. We both decided to hope for the best. I started and it went! But there's a happy ending to the story because, having effectively condemned Ian Holloway's Leicester to the drop, we ensured our survival by beating Norwich 4-1 at Hillsborough on the last day. I was gutted that I couldn't play because of the hamstring but it was a fantastic occasion with 36,000 in the ground. And what made it all the more special was that the lads gave me a guard of honour on the field at the end.

Coming to England had been about testing myself and my ambitions. I feel I more than passed that test. After promotion in my first season there was the question of whether this versatile veteran could match up to the Championship. Well, I did and for three seasons. It was great knowing that I could hold my own there. That gave me a great deal of satisfaction. Players can hit all sorts of peaks in their careers but the big challenge is ... can they stay there? Consistency is everything and I felt more than fulfilled over coming to England.

However, if it's about standing still in one sense, it's decidedly not in another. It's part of my nature, a product of my upbringing, that I'm always on the go, never idle.

Maybe sometimes I take on a bit too much. Certainly, that could have been said about this time in my life. I was at a stage where I had to look ahead, of course, and that meant creating some options inside and outside the game.

I took my UEFA 'A' licence with a view to coaching and also enrolled on a sports media degree course at Staffordshire University. This was run by a former Wednesday player, Lawrie Madden, who had built himself a media career. I was among the first intake of players along with people like Scott Minto. I was covering all bases and it meant a tough couple of years. It was manic at times. I was always on the move.

Having so much going on at the same time undoubtedly put a strain on my marriage. Kerry, as I've explained, was still living with the kids up in Scotland. We were officially divorced in 2008. I suppose I could easily put it down to the geographical distance between us and being apart. But the plain fact is that it was my fault. I wouldn't have wanted it to happen and yet it did. I will always look back with regret that I hurt somebody emotionally through no fault of their own. Kerry was and still is a fantastic mother. There were some tough times; a great deal of upset and a lot of guilt on my part. Thankfully we have managed to put it behind us. We never went through the courts and while my kids still live with Kerry, I have access to them all the time. We both tried to protect them as much as possible through the heartache. I'm also glad that Kerry is happily married again now just as I am settled with my partner Nicola. And all four of us get on well together.

It's not through any lack of sensitivity that I say I'd like to think the personal upset didn't affect me. I'd never blame the turmoil for errors on the park. Maybe subconsciously you struggle a little but I always kept my family business private.

At one stage towards the end of my final Hillsborough season Brian Laws told me about an opportunity to go to Port Vale on loan. If it had been a permanent move I might have thought about it, but I didn't want to miss out on the battle to avoid relegation.

I look back thinking that, come the summer, staying in England might have been the better option. Port Vale were still in for me along with a few other lower league clubs. But seeing more of the kids was a massive factor pulling me back to Scotland. Another was the persistence of Falkirk and their manager John Hughes. John, or Yogi as he's called,' had been after me for a while. For two or three years in fact.

Like the Canadian Mounties, he eventually got his man. Falkirk were in the Scottish Premier League and I was offered a two-year contract. Small club that they were, they had big ambitions and a brand new stadium. The facilities made it a bigger club than it was. But above all, I felt welcome and wanted.

18

Falkirk: More Final Heartbreak but the Goal of My Life

Far be it from me to give anyone a history lesson, even on my chosen subject. But would I be right, dear reader, that you might need a little brushing up on your knowledge of Falkirk Football Club? All right, no problem. Definitely not offended. Outside of Celtic and Rangers, I'd guess most English supporters don't know much about Scottish football. And vice versa. The big English clubs attract global attention but north of the border there isn't a lot of attention paid to many of the others.

Mention of Falkirk often prompts a few eyes to glaze over. Everyone knows the name, of course, but not a great deal more besides. So let's start with the fact that 'The Bairns', as they are called, are a very old established club dating back to 1876. As such, they have a rich tradition. In the earlier years Falkirk were twice runners-up to champions Celtic, pipped for the title in 1908 and 1910. Fast upon that, the club won the Scottish Cup in 1913; later to repeat the feat in 1957.

And Falkirk hold a joint record for winning the second tier, achieving promotion that way on seven occasions, which,– at the time of writing,– was matched only by St.

Johnstone. Their last spell of top flight football came via promotion in 2005 and Falkirk had the honour of playing in the inaugural UEFA Europa League in 2009-10 during my time with them.

So what you have is a small club that's big on achievement. Thinks big, too. Hence the new stadium I referred to previously. In all, Falkirk have had five homes since their formation. They began at Hope Street before playing at Randyford Park and then Blinkbonny Park. Get those names, by the way. From 1885, The Bairns spent more than a century at Brockville Park, which was built on the former Hope Street ground. Come the formation of the Scottish Premier League, the old place did not conform to strict stadium criteria. Sadly, that cost the club promotion to the top flight on three occasions. Enough was enough. Cue pastures new. The Falkirk Stadium is a 9,200 capacity all-seater stadium on the outskirts of town. It has been the club's proud home since 2004-05 when the team celebrated with promotion in its first season there.

When I joined them in the summer of 2008 Falkirk were really fancying having a go at getting in the top six. They'd been falling just short, so the feeling was that a bit more experience in the squad would see them over the line. To that end they signed three other players, apart from me, to add know-how to the team. Two of them were big names in Scotland. There was Jackie McNamara, the ex-Celtic star, signed from Aberdeen and Neil McCann, formerly of Rangers, who arrived from Hearts. Joining them was my old Sheffield Wednesday team-mate Burton O'Brien, who moved back to Scotland from Hillsborough.

It was to be a season of drama and heartbreak. What is it with me and cup competitions? Anyway, we'll come to that. We had a fantastic pre-season with everyone very positive.

That mood carried over into our first game of the campaign and you couldn't get a bigger one than being at home to Rangers. We played tremendously well but still lost 1-0 after Michael Higdon missed a penalty. Rangers scored a late winner and you had to hand it to them in a sense. Big teams always seem to find a way of winning. It's what makes them successful I suppose. Maybe it's a question of belief and expectation.

To put it into context, Falkirk is a small town with a population of just around 34,000. It's about the same size as somewhere like Worksop in Nottinghamshire, near to my base in Sheffield. Falkirk is bang in between Glasgow and Edinburgh so it is hemmed in by four big clubs. I'd imagine the majority of the fans are born and brought up in the town. There isn't much support from outside. Our crowds had a lower base of 3,000 and when you think about it, that is very good. It means that 10% of the population are turning out to support the team come hell or high water.

I had my ups and downs with the manager, John Hughes. He could be quite fanatical, certainly very strong in his views. We had run-ins where I felt he was in the wrong but I did respect him and his way of playing. John was also one of those types I'd come across before who would use me, being a very experienced player, as a battering ram at times.

Sometimes you deserve it and you're the first to know yourself if you do. But I knew that he was picking me out as a psychological ploy aimed at the other players. If it happened to me, it could certainly happen to them. And it served as a warning to the younger lads to get their fingers out. Remember how I used to go into my shell as a younger player … by now it was water off a duck's back. I really liked John's training methods and his philosophy on how the game should be played. It was very much a footballing approach, adopting a Dutch-style 4-3-3 system. I liked to play a passing game, even as a defender by now, and the training was always focused on work with the ball. In fact, I took a lot of John's ideas into my later work with the kids at Wednesday.

I started out at right back with Falkirk and switched between there and centre half. Finishing in a perilous 10th place was a bitter disappointment but it made for a very exciting last game of the season. We travelled to Inverness Caledonian Thistle needing to win to ensure we stayed in the SPL. The Highland people are very strong and this was a tough, tough game. Besides, they had Terry Butcher as manager. Butcher was bravery personified as a lion-hearted England defender and teams tend to adopt the character of their boss. This was a test of character for us and it was one we passed. A goal from Michael Higdon, making up for his penalty miss on the first day of the season, saw us to a 1-0 victory.

The other highlights were runs in both cup competitions. Unfortunately, Rangers did for us on both occasions. They beat us 3-0 in a League Cup semi-final at Hampden and were lying in wait again when we reached the final of the Scottish Cup. This was after we'd beaten my former team Dunfermline in the semis. By this stage, I'd become something of a bit part player. I'd been dropped but got on from the bench against Dunfermline. The biggest thing in my favour was my versatility once again and I felt this would secure me a place among the substitutes for the final. I didn't expect to start but felt I deserved to be on the bench. It seemed to be between me and Steven Pressley. Considering he played in just the one position as a centre back I felt fairly confident.

Like me, Steven was in his veteran years. He came out

and said that the final would be his swansong and that he'd retire from playing after the game. Whether that emotional backdrop affected the manager's decision, I don't know. We weren't told the team until the day of the game. When it was read out and I wasn't named as one of the substitutes, I felt some eyes turning towards me. It wasn't just me feeling I deserved to be on the bench. Quite a few of the lads were disappointed for me. But I handled the disappointment differently to the previous occasion when I missed out on a big day. I concentrated on supporting the lads and once again we played really well, giving Rangers a hell of a run for their money. It took an absolute wonder strike to beat us. Nacho Novo, who'd scored twice against us in the League Cup, surpassed himself with one of the best goals I've seen. The Spanish star had only been on the field for a few seconds after leaving the bench when he hit a ferocious volley from fully 40 yards. It flew past our keeper Dani Mallo. Game over. Always the bridesmaids.

John Hughes decided to move on that summer. He went to manage Hibernian, the team he played for. That was just too big a draw for John – who had green blood running through his veins. The board promoted a guy called Eddie May who was our academy coach and had done a great job with the kids. A new management team was put around Eddie. He had two assistants in Steven Pressley and the vastly experienced former St Mirren and Aberdeen manager Alex Smith, who was regarded as the godfather of Scottish football.

I still had a year left on contract and had no thoughts other than playing. There was nothing else in the air, as far as I knew, when Eddie pulled me in and said that he wasn't going to play me in the forthcoming season. Instead, he asked if I'd be interested in taking over as youth coach. It was, to say the least, a wee bit of a surprise. I was presented with the sort of decision I'd like to have made a year later. But in hindsight Eddie gave me an opportunity at a good time. I was now 38, after all, and it was important to have a foot in the door of coaching.

But I never announced anything to the effect that I was hanging up my boots. That became significant because, after a few injuries, I was asked to stick the shirt on again. I played half a dozen times and there was a memorable occasion when I was thrown on up front. This was against Hamilton and it provided what, for many fans, was the highlight of my time with Falkirk. I'm reminded of it on Twitter to this day.

What happened? Well, all modesty aside, I have to admit I scored a fantastic goal. Hamilton were playing a big offside trap on the halfway line and I was on the ball with one centre half heading towards me and the other right beside me. I just set off on this great run. The defender heading my way stood off and stood off. I think he fancied I'd miss anyway. Certainly, there was still a lot to do when I ended up at the edge of the area one-on-one with the keeper. Having run from the halfway line, I thought 'I've just got to take this one.' I've never hit a ball sweeter in my life. It flew into the top corner and that was 2-0 game over.

Poor Eddie May didn't even have a full season in charge. I was gutted for Eddie when he left, having got on really well with him. It was results related, of course, but all the same this can be a cruel business. I was glad to see Eddie go to Rangers as a youth coach and I think he may have been relieved to get the pressure off. This was a big turning point for me and the club. Falkirk promoted Steven Pressley to manage the team and also appointed me as his assistant. We still got relegated but that is only half the story. Having been something like eight points adrift at one stage, we took the fight right to the last day.

The credit for that must go to Steven. After taking the job, he made a big announcement to the media that was bold and brave. Steven told the world that we would not go down. This rubbed up other clubs the wrong way. There was a lot of negativity towards us and it created a siege mentality. But I genuinely think that Steven did the right thing. It changed the mood of the club and got the right reaction from the players.

They were thinking: 'Well, he believes in us so let's give it a right go.' And they did. Some critics thought Steven showed inexperience in the way he went about it and he took a bit of stick. But the reality is that he almost achieved a miracle. We clawed our way back to the extent that we could have stayed up by winning at Kilmarnock in our last game. In the event, the 0-0 draw kept Killies up and put us down. We had a golden chance, though, with a few minutes to go. Ryan Flynn, later to join Sheffield United, won't thank me for mentioning that it fell to him. He put it over the bar. Such are the slim margins in football.

19

Plotting Rangers' Downfall on £350 a Week (Before Tax)

Picking up here with Falkirk. So we were relegated from the SPL. Let me tell you exactly what that means. In England we're used to the Premiership being the be-all and end-all. The difference is probably even greater in Scotland because the finance up there has essentially revolved around just two clubs. If you're not playing Celtic and Rangers, plus the TV money that goes with it, then you are cut adrift from the revenue stream. Not only did Falkirk lose the Old Firm games but also the Dunfermline derby as my old team were promoted. Considering the small size of the club in the first place the downsizing had to be drastic.

Just how drastic may shock you. No messing around here. The team budget had to be cut by 75%. Not over a period but straightaway. We got rid of nearly everyone. About 15 players, obviously including the best ones, left that summer. Among those Scott Arfield joined Huddersfield Town. Later, Arfield would be followed to the Terriers by two more of Falkirk's finest, Kallum Higginbotham and Murray Wallace. What did we do about it? Well, what could we do? We just put the kids in. By the time I left to come back south the average age of the squad was around 19. We had 16 year olds turning out for us and I mean regularly.

As for the coaching staff, well, we all took a huge hit in the pocket. Effectively, I was out of a job. My playing deal had expired. Although I'd become assistant manager I had no contract covering this. It was a bit of a limbo situation all round because I'd never at any stage said that my playing career was over. You don't want to go slamming doors behind you because you never know when they might creak open again, creak being the word as I was now 39 years of age!

That summer, I decided my future with my heart rather than my head. I stayed on as assistant to the manager, Steven Pressley, and ended up taking a wage cut of 82%. Yes, you read that right. 82%.

Normally, I wouldn't bandy around my exact earnings but it might be necessary to do that here in order to put that drop into perspective. I have to do so really because it affected my future and the decision I took in my second season coaching with Falkirk in the Scottish First Division. When I was playing with the club in the SPL my deal worked out at roughly £100,000 a year. It was really good money. Maybe the bonuses were bigger when I was at Sheffield Wednesday but my Falkirk wages were on a par with my best earnings elsewhere. From £100,000 I went down to £18,000. That's a huge drop in anyone's language. I've always been reasonably careful with cash but everyone adjusts their lifestyle to what they earn. Most people, whatever they are paid, would struggle to cope with a drop of 82%.

So life was a real struggle on and off the pitch in season 2010-11. Not that I was on the field myself. I just don't think it's possible to combine the jobs of playing and coaching, let alone player-managing. Coaching demands 100% if you are doing it properly. I know there are many examples of people doing both roles towards the end of their careers but I don't feel it's realistic to give your best in either job. Apart from any other consideration, I don't think it's fair on the players.

Anyway, we had a decent season all the same, finishing third. Just one promotion place, remember, so it's tough getting back to the SPL. I thought that to finish so high with a bunch of kids was one hell of an achievement. It was a quick growing-up exercise and I'd have to say the squad over-performed that year. Our crowds held up well, too. I see the average for the season was over 4,000. Not bad at all. But the supporters did become a touch greedy. Some of them forgot all about the cuts and the age of the team, thinking we should have bounced straight back. It was never going to be that easy. Expectations were also raised by an outstanding run in the Scottish League Cup. We beat Hearts 4-3 at home to reach the quarter-finals before dipping out at Aberdeen in a highly respectable 2-1 defeat.

This was a foretaste of the following campaign when Falkirk achieved one of the best results in their history. It was the season I left the club but not before I had shared in some pretty sensational goings-on. Not so in the league where the team went on to finish third for a second time after I'd left. It was again a decent showing with what we had, but the average league attendance of just over 3,000 reflected the mood of the fans. That said, we gave them all something to remember until their dying day with another run in the League Cup that reached incredible heights.

There was no warning of what was to come when we won 4-2 at Albion Rovers in the first round and accounted for Stenhousemuir 3-1 at home in the second. But those victories set up a third round home tie with the mighty

Rangers on September 21st, 2011. Some dates are never to be forgotten. This was one of them. Certainly, the 6,493 people who witnessed the occasion will always remember it.

It was a fairytale from the start. We played 4-5-1 but you'd never have known it. Two great headers from Farid El Alagui gave the Bairns a 2-0 lead. The second of those was set up by a cross from a lad called Craig Sibbald who was just 16 at the time. He was one of four teenagers in the side. Our fans were in dreamland. It was then that the Rangers manager Ally McCoist brought on his big guns, not that he hadn't started with a strong line-up. Nikica Jelavic and Steven Naismith came off the bench to crank up the pressure. Dorin Goian pulled one back for the Gers and it was Jelavic who equalised for 2-2. Remarkably, all four goals in the game had been headers but then this was no ordinary contest.

As full-time approached our lads were out on their feet. Had it gone into extra-time I reckon we'd have ended up losing by something like 5-2. But we got a free-kick near the box in injury time and Mark Millar scored from it to give us an epic 3-2 triumph. Millar's shot caught out the Rangers keeper Neil Alexander. He could only push it onto the bar and into the net. Millar had been on Celtic's books as a kid – you couldn't make any of this up. The fans went berserk. You think to yourself : Is this really happening? Nothing beats playing, of course, but this was one of my biggest highs in football.

McCoist pulled no punches in his criticism of Rangers' players but said: 'We put out a team that should have been good enough to win the game and they didn't. It's to Falkirk's credit that they're through.'

It's also worth recalling Steven Pressley's reaction which summed up everything perfectly from our point of view:

'I can't praise my players enough. I'm so proud of them. Their belief and composure under pressure was remarkable for such a young side. Our supporters have got to bask in this, a wonderful result. For Rangers to come back and level the game, you'd normally expect the more experienced and stronger team to win. But the young players showed remarkable mentality. They played like men.'

And there was more. Somehow we also won away to Dundee United in the quarter-finals. This was to be my last game and the lads knew I was leaving. More on that later, but what a way to go out. I couldn't have asked for anything better. It took 70 minutes for the deadlock to be broken and once again we took the lead with a header from Farid El Alagui, his 15th goal in 16 games for us. Johnny Russell levelled for United almost immediately to send the tie into extra time whereupon Jon Daly put the home team in front. But substitute Ally Graham levelled for us in the 118th minute. Cue a penalty shoot-out which we edged 5-4. Willo Flood missed for them, ballooning over the bar, and Stewart Murdoch kept his cool to send us through.

Once again Steven Pressley's reputation was enhanced, especially his ability to work on the proverbial shoestring. Our director of football Alex Smith paid tribute to Steven, saying: 'He has the ability and the temperament to be the manager of a big club. He's got a big future in front of him.'

I enjoyed working with Steven. He has a big personality, isn't scared of making enemies, and just wants to be successful. I always wondered if he might get the opportunity of coming to an English club at some stage. That actually happened early in 2013 when he became manager of Coventry City, a famous club struggling against financial problem. It would have been a tall order for anybody but jobs like these nearly always come up at the least opportune times. Steven did not want to regret spurning such a chance at some stage in the future. I wish him well. We had a fantastic relationship and people often ask me if we might link up again sometime. In fact, there was some serious talk about me joining him at Coventry, although the timing wasn't right. As for the future, well, everybody harbours ambition and I would certainly look at the possibility of working with Steven again if it ever came up. That said, it would take an extremely good offer for me to leave Sheffield Wednesday where I am very happy and settled for the foreseeable future.

Leaving Falkirk after the Dundee United victory meant I missed out on our semi-final at Hampden Park in which we finally bowed out 3-1 to Celtic. Why did I go at that point? Well, it was purely about money – or the lack of it. I just couldn't afford to live on what I was being paid in Scotland. I think the low level of pay in Scottish football is an eye-opener to people in England. You'd earn more up there playing part-time.

That's why Scottish players, and some managers too, are desperate to get to England. Finance isn't the only factor, though. There's another and it's a very big one called boredom. In Scotland you play the same team so often you get sick of the sight of each other. I remember at Falkirk going to Partick Thistle nine times in the one season – the four league games plus five more visits in cup competitions. I'd say that's the number one reason players want to come to England, even more than the money.

The Old Firm games are nearly all that's left up there and with Rangers having been relegated to the bottom division because of their financial collapse, Scottish football is in a real mess right now. The game up there is paying the price for greed in my opinion. A few years ago the powers that be jumped out of bed with Sky TV to go with ITV Digital, which then collapsed. So who is the next saviour? Right, Setanta – and they go bust. It means Scottish football has had to go back cap in hand to Sky who effectively can now screen games for whatever they're prepared to offer.

There's been a frightening drop in standards north of the board. At one time there would be international class players. You think of people such as Henrik Larsson, Mikel Arteta and the de Boer brothers, Frank and Ronald. Nowadays Celtic are having to buy players from the Championship and below, which is no disrespect to the likes of Gary Hooper who has shown himself to be a fine striker at Parkhead. That's why it was such a phenomenal achievement for Celtic to win through to the last 16 of the Champions League in 2012-13.

The talk persists of the Glasgow clubs joining up with the Premiership as a sort of British league. But that has become unrealistic because of the drop in standard in Scotland and, of course, the demise (albeit temporary perhaps) of Rangers. Nevertheless there is a real desire to team up with the English game in general. If you offered Celtic and Rangers the chance to start all the way down in League Two, would they take it? I honestly think they would. They would then back themselves, with their vast support, to come all the way through the leagues. That would also end all the arguments about the two Welsh sides, Swansea and Cardiff, playing in England. Both are in the Premier League as we speak following Cardiff's promotion in 2013.

As for me, it was a no-brainer to come back south. Even here, people have this misconception about what footballers earn. They seem to think that anybody in the game – even at, say, Bury or Rochdale – is automatically a millionaire. Players have women throwing themselves at them. It's only when they step out to the car park and see a Peugeot instead of a Porsche that they realise the truth.

The fact is that all my savings had just disappeared. It was partly my own fault that I had just been through a divorce. But I was no different to anyone else in having a couple of young kids, a mortgage to pay and a car to run. It was impossible to make ends meet so I headed south for a fresh start in football and a new business venture.

20

The Businessman Coach

Sheffield is a fairly closely-guarded secret when it comes to its residential delights. But its appeal has not escaped the host of sporting luminaries who have set up home there over recent times. They have found fashionable houses and beautiful countryside at unfashionable prices. Am I beginning to sound a bit like an estate agent? Well, I'm coming to that! Certainly there is far more – shall I say – potential in the steel city as a place to live than the popular image of industrial grime would suggest. That might still be the predominant view of those bypassing Sheffield on the M1 at the east end of town. But if you cross to the west and south there is tree-lined suburbia bordering the Peak District. I'm starting to like this brochure, one of my best I reckon!

Okay, I'm a convert as a Sheffield resident, especially one who now has houses to sell. But don't take it from me. Ask Chris Waddle who came to the city towards the end of his illustrious playing career, became a Sheffield Wednesday legend and has never moved away. Chris is as Geordie as they come but he and his family have made Sheffield their home. The late Emlyn Hughes felt the same affinity, staying well beyond his fleeting spell as manager of nearby Rotherham United. And they tell me Dave Bassett, your typical Londoner, liked the place so much that he and his family remained in Sheffield for some years after his managerial era at Bramall Lane. I also know that Trevor Francis felt a similar attachment during and after being a player and boss at Hillsborough.

Besides, Sheffield was the home since boyhood of the great athlete Sebastian Coe. Olympic golden girl Jessica Ennis was born and raised in a city that took her to its heart long before the nation's embrace. World squash champion Nick Matthew is another proud Sheffielder while celebrated former England cricket captain – and avid Owls fan – Michael Vaughan, made it his adopted city. For many years, Sheffield has also been the powerbase of English football, boasting Premier League chief Sir Dave Richards, ex-FA chairman Geoff Thompson in his time at the Sheffield and Hallamshire FA, and former referees' manager Keith Hackett.

I could go on but you get the picture. Not that any of this was the reason why I came back down from Scotland, but the 'venus flytrap' appeal of Sheffield is certainly helping me build a new life. I returned with nothing concrete on the football horizon, although I had kept in touch with Wednesday's academy manager Sean McAuley. I'd always got on very well with Sean and he said he hoped to get me involved somehow. Where I *was* seriously involved, on both a personal and professional level, was with my partner Nicola. Her parents had created and built up the estate agency (Spencers) that bore their name. They were ready to retire from the business and, to cut a long story short, we bought it off them. Effectively, we pooled our resources to do the deal and, of course, the terms were favourable because naturally Mr. and Mrs. Spencer were delighted to keep the business in the family and wanted their daughter to succeed.

Nicola knew the trade inside-out whereas I was a total novice. Her parents had run it very successfully, although maybe this was also the perfect time with the business approaching its 20th anniversary for Nicola to give it a kick up the backside. She set about re-branding the company through a website and use of the modern media. It was really her baby. We went 50-50 with the purchase but she's the gaffer having had more than a dozen years experience. Me, I'm more of an office manager type role. I do a lot of the admin, chasing up debts and keeping the paperwork in order. Nicola is the one who's out doing the valuations.

We took over at a difficult time in the middle of a recession but things are going well. The aim was to break even over the first couple of years and now we're expanding. We've taken over the lease of the office next to us and there's new signage going up. It's quite an exciting time. I've always loved learning new things and never been afraid of hard work.

While nothing can beat the thrill of football, it's very satisfying work. I speak having seen the other side of the property world in dealing with repossessions with Alliance and Leicester. Now it's lovely when people come in with a box of chocolates because they want to say thanks for helping their move go smoothly. It's also a great feeling to close a deal and see the profits going up. Property is very cyclical. Nobody buys houses over Christmas or during the summer holidays but there are good sales at other times. We're also aiming to have 50 to 100 properties that we can look after on behalf of landlords and rent out. This provides a steady income.

Although I moved into a full-time coaching role with Wednesday after buying the estate agency with Nicola, I feel there is a great balance between the two. I still have a lot of commitment and responsibility towards the company. It's important that I show I'm not just using it as a toy. We had to start by cutting the staff and costs right down. As we build it back up we might be able to increase staff numbers again. As I write this, we have seven full-timers. There might be an opportunity in future to delegate certain jobs so that I can get even more involved in football.

I take no salary out of the company and Nicola takes just a basic wage. While we are expanding, most of the profits are being ploughed back in. I think it's been good for me to know what life is like in the real world after my experiences at both ends of my career. I only had a relatively short time in what I call 'the bubble.'

Looking back, it might have been a good thing that the football side of my life was in limbo around the time we took control of the business. It gave me the breathing space to adjust to something new. But I stayed in touch with the game and made what turned out to be a very fruitful call one day to an old mate from Scotland, Ross Wilson.

Ross was in a backroom role with Watford under their then manager Sean Dyche, having done a similar job at Falkirk. I phoned him to ask for some tickets for a game. He said he could do better than that and promptly offered me a bit of scouting work. This involved watching future opponents or prospective signings and writing reports. It was great because it kept me in the loop.

Another new departure came via an invitation from my co-author Alan Biggs to write a regular column for the weekly Sheffield Telegraph newspaper. This was a forum for my views on the Owls and it couldn't have come at a more dramatic or exciting time. First, there was the shock of a manager change when Gary Megson was dismissed within days of a Sheffield derby victory over United at Hillsborough.

As harsh as this seemed at the time, Gary's replacement, Dave Jones, then had the team roaring away to automatic promotion at the climax of a thrilling head-to-head race with the Blades. Of course I had many connections, not to mention friends, at Hillsborough and I had to marry diplomacy with putting forward an honest opinion. I think I achieved this difficult balancing act as no relationships were compromised and I learned that opinions are fine – we all have them – as long as they are put across in a constructive manner.

Also, there are times when you have to take a step back from going overboard either in praise or criticism. Gary's departure was an example of that. At the time, fans were angry with the club's owner Milan Mandaric and threatening to turn against the man whose timely takeover had saved the Owls from going out of business. It's important to keep things in perspective. As unfortunate and harsh as the decision looked (and I still think Gary did a very good job for the club), Milan obviously had his reasons and he was ultimately vindicated by the success of Dave Jones. At the end of the season there could only be praise for both managers and chairman.

At Wednesday Sean had kept me in mind and he was as good as his word when some jobs came up in the academy network. It meant I could go back to Hillsborough as, and this might impress you, an SPDC. To give it the full works, the job title was Senior Professional Development Coach. I'll explain exactly what that means in a later chapter.

Another of the balls I had in the air at this time was my coaching badges and I was determined to get the full set. I duly completed my UEFA A and B badges and was working towards my Pro Licence, which I went on to achieve at the start of 2013. Hey folks, that means I can officially coach Barcelona in the Champions League if given the opportunity! Some people think it's just about putting the cones out. They couldn't be more wrong. The Pro Licence is almost like taking a university degree. I think this sort of in-depth preparation is necessary in the modern game because managers have to deal with an incredible amount of stuff.

Just think for a moment about the different aspects of the game and you'll come up with all the many areas the Pro Licence covers. Here are some of the subject areas:

- Man-management
- Dealing with the chairman and attending board meetings
- Handling agents
- Learning effective video analysis techniques
- Negotiating transfers
- Operating to a budget
- Coping with the demands of the media

Wrapped around this was a study of individual managers, players and teams. For instance, I went to the European Under-21 championships in Denmark as part of the course and also spent five days with a club in Portugal. Then there were lectures from luminaries such as Sir Alex Ferguson, Marcello Lippi, David Moyes and Andre Villas-Boas. I came out of it all with a full-sized book summarising everything I'd learned. It was a truly educational experience and one that's worth looking at in more detail.

21

Back to School – with the Best Teacher of them All

The Pro Licence isn't just an education. It's an experience to be treasured. I came out with so much more than a piece of paper, even if that qualification technically entitled me to take on any managerial or coaching role in the world of football. This is all a reflection on how much the culture surrounding the game is changing. For previous generations, the football pitch and the classroom could not be further apart. They were in different galaxies of the universal life experience.

The traditional background of the professional player was a kid who ignored his studies at school and only took an interest in games lessons. He'd leave with few qualifications other than his ability to kick a ball. To some extent, this can still be true today but it is actively discouraged by the game itself. Club academies run education programmes so that the lads who miss out on a football career at least have some other options.

You'll recall how this was so important to me at the start of my career when I was able to get a job with Alliance and Leicester to support my ambitions as a part-time player. There was no other way I could have made my career unfold as it has done. Even in that relatively short time-span there have been big changes in football's relationship with education as a whole. Not only are kids encouraged with their studies but football has become an academic subject in its own right.

The game has become more technical and scientific. There is still simplicity at its heart but complexity in the tactics. For instance, World champions Spain won EURO 2012 playing such a sophisticated passing game that on occasions they operated without a recognised striker. How on earth did they manage that? Commonly, at the very top of the game, teams will have only one forward player. There is a tendency to thread telling passes through the middle rather than play the ball out wide for crosses into the box. It makes you think, and coaches can never stop doing that if they are to keep pace with the development of the game and maybe find some innovations of their own.

I took the Pro Licence course through the Scottish Football Association. It lasted from January 2011 to October 2012 and the time lapse alone will tell you of the amount of ground we covered. 'We' comprised a group of 23 of us. Among them were former Everton and Scotland midfielder Stuart McCall, who had coached at Sheffield United before going on to manage Motherwell. There was ex-Rangers captain and Everton stalwart David Weir. In fact, ex-Evertonians abounded considering that Alan Stubbs and David Unsworth were also on the course. Others included former Preston and Burnley legend Graham Alexander, who played beyond the age of 40, and Anna Signuel, head coach of the Scotland women's team.

One of our opening lectures came from John Hughes who I much admired from my time of playing under him at Falkirk. John, just a few months into a tough new job at Hartlepool as I write this, is an example of the old saying that you should never judge a book by its cover. To those who don't really know him he might come across as rough and aggressive. He's not either of those things, just very passionate about the way he feels the game should be played. And again, contrary to the myth, he swears by passing football and his overall belief in a 4-3-3 system. Personally, I'm a great believer in being able to adapt or change if things are not going right on the day, but I fully respect John's approach and it's only by hearing the other side of the argument that you can fully form your own views.

A quote from John's talk that really struck a chord with me was this one: 'You are at your strongest when you first get the job.' This could be said to refer to what is commonly called the honeymoon period after a manager is first appointed. I've seen that time and again over my career where managers have come in and made an impact.

But John was also referring to something deeper here. When he was at Falkirk he had a free hand with the club's whole football operation, from the academy to the first team and from the training facilities to the choice of kit. He had a good relationship with those above him and felt that his power base enabled him to be relatively successful at Falkirk.

When he moved to Hibernian, John had no say in many aspects of the club's operation. He couldn't impose his philosophy on future players and his responsibilities were confined to the first team, yet without any influence over the football budget. John also felt he learned from the fact that he inherited the club's existing coaching staff. He felt he never had full support and issues of trust began to arise when results went against the team.

John posed the question to us: 'Do you take your own

staff when you have the power to do so, or do you work with inherited staff?' He didn't give an answer of his own but the unmistakable impression was that he'd have done the former with the benefit of hindsight. John's pay-off line was this: 'You are at your strongest when you're first in the job. Get everything you can at that time.'

What you see is what you get with John Hughes. He wears his heart on his sleeve and had two totally conflicting experiences at Falkirk and Hibernian. His presentation perfectly illustrated some of the obstacles strewn across the path of management. There was a sense of pride about his time at Falkirk and a feeling of disappointment about his Hibs experience. This did make me wonder, as it did at the time, whether his decision to take the job at Easter Road where he'd been a player, came from his heart or his head. The lesson for me was that emotional attachment is not necessarily the best way to go when considering an offer.

With no disrespect to anyone, when managers at all levels want advice there is one man and one man alone they probably think of first. Not everyone has a direct line to him, of course, but the man in question has always been renowned for returning calls and offering words of wisdom to people right across his profession. He is Sir Alex Ferguson, the greatest manager of the modern age and arguably the greatest of all time. The Pro Licence course was the vehicle that took us for a day's visit to Carrington, the great man's training base at Manchester United. And built into the schedule was this ... 10.30am: Forum with Sir Alex Ferguson. It was to last through until midday. Imagine that, 90 minutes – the equivalent of a whole match – to quiz the undisputed master of football management. Naturally, we seized our opportunity in a wide-ranging discussion.

With hindsight, the session was even more valuable

bearing in mind Sir Alex's decision to stand down at the end of last season. He did so after collecting his 13th league title. If that was not phenomenal enough, he won 36 trophies in his 26 years at Old Trafford. These are breathtaking statistics, none more so than the last figure mentioned above.

To be in charge of Manchester United for more than a quarter of a century is absolutely remarkable. I cannot see this ever being repeated at a major club, let alone all the silverware. Of course, to reign for so long Sir Alex had to deliver on a fairly regular basis. But it should never be forgotten how United backed him through the troublesome transition of his early years with the club. There is an unmissable lesson there for the game as a whole. Or should be.

And so to the grand tour of Fergie's empire. First let me take you inside the training centre, located near a village off the M60 motorway. The media have dubbed it 'Fortress Carrington' due to the 1.5 miles of fencing and 30,000 trees surrounding it. Inside the complex – screened off from journalists and opposition spies – are training, rehabilitation, physiotherapy and massage areas plus hydrotherapy pools. Aside from 14 football pitches of varying sizes, there are also squash and basketball courts. Let's see, what else? Yes, a sauna and weight rooms, a restaurant, conference rooms, offices, classrooms and a television studio for interviews with players and staff on MUTV. It's the works.

The first thing that Sir Alex Ferguson talked about became the overriding piece of advice that was to stick in my head more than anything else. There was much, much more, of course, but a few simple words at the start really resonated with me. He told us: 'The standards are very, very important … do not EVER drop your standards. That is something your players will always respect.'

What he meant, among other things, was that coaching sessions must be well prepared and have structure and organisation about them. Sir Alex also stressed that managers and coaches should look to learn from their players. One example he related was of something he picked up from Eric Cantona who was the first player – after a session – to ask to borrow a couple of players to stay out on the pitch and cross balls for him. That practice is now a regular part of player development at Carrington. For instance, David Beckham and Cristiano Ronaldo would both practise their free-kicks for an extra half-hour after training. Sir Alex made the point that 'players must learn something from every training session, no matter how small it seems.'

Another pearl of wisdom was Sir Alex's stipulation that a coach should be very sparing with the use of his own voice. He reflected that as a younger manager at Aberdeen he would get totally involved in training, shouting, pointing and giving orders. Then one day his assistant, Archie Knox, turned to him and said: 'What did you learn from that session?' It was only then that the young Ferguson realised that he'd been involved in the session to such a degree that he wasn't able to watch it properly.

This led to questions about what Sir Alex looked for in appointing his assistants. At Aberdeen he made a play initially for Walter Smith for his 'structure and discipline' but couldn't get him and went instead for Pat Stanton. This was despite the fact that Stanton 'had a different personality to me, low key, quiet voice and strong opinions.' When Stanton moved on, Sir Alex brought in Knox who had 'great enthusiasm and work ethic.'

Then, on moving to Manchester United, he wanted an assistant from within the club and installed Brian Kidd whose sessions 'always had a good structure about them.'

It seemed that Sir Alex had no hard and fast rules in this area, being able to work with different personalities. He summed up that he'd been very lucky with his assistants and seemed to be quite good at picking the right people.

Sir Alex also blew away some of the myths about players kicking up over squad rotation, simply saying: 'If we are winning silverware nobody complains and in the modern game it's impossible to keep the same team.'

Qualifying for Europe is obviously the number one demand on any Manchester United team, as he acknowledged. It meant that Sir Alex would prioritise his selections towards big European games rather than big league games towards the end of the season. He told us: 'We always look three games ahead when planning our starting eleven.'

Selection factors include the use of sports science to understand how players are feeling. Not that Sir Alex professed himself to be an expert in this area, quipping: 'I'm a dinosaur when it comes to technology!' He also stood by old fashioned methods – which are seen to stand the test of time in his case – when it came to assessing what he saw in front of him in matches. He said 'I never make notes during a game. I like to use the naked eye in my decision-making.'

So what did Sir Alex look for in up-and-coming talent, something he and Manchester United had long been renowned for developing?

'First and foremost it must be their ability,' he told us. 'After that it would be personality, character and upbringing.' He admitted that this was more difficult to check in the case of foreign players but also pointed to a culture change at home. Sir Alex explained: 'A lot of the modern day kids that are coming into our academy are very fragile and the parents are very hands-on in the hope that they can live their dreams through their kids. We have to do regular reports for parents and deal with welfare officers, basically mollycoddle a lot of the youths today.'

Sir Alex, though, was clearly a manager who had successfully adapted his methods. He is famed, of course, for his supposed 'hairdryer' treatment in post-match inquests. We asked if he had changed in the way he reacted to a poor performance.

'I've probably mellowed with age a little bit,' he said. 'But in general I deal with things in the same way. I get it out my system immediately after the game, then it's done, dusted and we move on. If a player has not performed to a standard and done things he's not supposed to, I will let him know.'

That said, Sir Alex placed a great emphasis on a trusting relationship with his players. For instance, he would grant a day off when requested without probing the player for a reason – unless they wished to tell him. He said: 'If one of my players needs help with something, I will never tell a soul about it because that is the trust you need to build up with your players.'

His advice for new coaches was that they must have a strong personality and behave in some ways like an old-fashioned schoolteacher.

'Always strive to be inspirational and see yourself in them, the players. NEVER change your discipline or code of conduct, the players see that right away and double standards will destroy your relationship with your players.'

Another key relationship is that between a manager and his boss in the boardroom. Sir Alex was forced to heed some of the demarcation lines from an experience early in his career. He reflected that he learned a big lesson at St. Mirren through being stupid and naïve.

That arose because he 'wanted to do everything' including 'order pies and stationery.' Sir Alex's conclusion: 'I ruffled too many feathers and it cost me. Never educate directors on the game, it's dangerous! But always respect their position and never call the chairman by his first name, always Mr. Chairman.'

Similarly, Sir Alex had revised his previous habit of handling contract negotiations with players, based on his well-known contempt for agents and their demands, which he described as absolutely scandalous at times. The media is another area that always carries potential conflict, although Sir Alex had this golden rule when it comes to criticism:

'The first very important thing is not to take it personally as that is very dangerous.' Equally, he recognised that in the days of the 24 hour rolling media, newspapers are increasingly looking for 'the story behind the story.' Significantly, he added: 'Experience definitely helps you with interviews as you learn to listen and give yourself time to give a considered answer.'

So what gave Sir Alex the most satisfaction? 'Developing and improving players,' he said. 'We've had quite a few who've come through and gone on to be international stars.'

Now here's an extension to that comment that might surprise those who had this image of Sir Alex as a ruthless football manager. 'More importantly, it's about making them better people and I'd like to think that down the years we've helped mould players that carry themselves in the right manner and have a good character. I can't think of any that have disappointed me.'

But there is no room for sentiment when it comes to team selection. Sir Alex insisted that a manager must be able to make decisions and be ruthless for the good of the team. There is room for some humility, though. He added 'You will not get it right all the time so it is a good thing if you can hold your hand up and admit mistakes. Your players will respect that.'

Judgements do not come finer than recognising when players are past their best, something for which Sir Alex has become particularly acknowledged in making some tough but unfailingly accurate decisions.

'Your eyes never lie and you can see when players start to lose the hunger in their eyes so you must be ruthless,' he advised. 'Never create a "family" with your players, it makes decisions too difficult.'

Wow! What a goldmine of information and guidance. The 90 minutes flew by and, looking back, I think we put it to the best possible use. You can't put too high a value on the opportunity to learn from the best. Sir Alex's legacy to the game will be more than just the monumental success and lasting structure he left behind at Manchester United. It can also be measured in the vast knowledge he willingly imparts.

As an exercise for the course, I noted more than 20 points from Sir Alex which resonated with me and then produced a top ten:

- Discipline/code of conduct (relates to everyone, staff, players)
- Personality (be inspirational and enthusiastic)
- Character (mental toughness in difficult times)
- Structure (planning and preparation are vital for short and long term)
- Staff (choose people who complement you – and friends aren't always the best choice)
- Trust (never have double standards, players notice it)
- Respect (earn it, give it out)

- Work ethic (delegate but don't shirk responsibility)
- Be ruthless (when making decisions for the good of the team/ player)
- Strong opinions (you need to have them, your staff need to have them)

From Carrington it was north to Largs and the SportScotland National Centre. There we had an extensive tutorial from the FA's elite coaching manager Dick Bate, a vastly experienced guy who, among other things, has coached at Leeds and been in charge of the England youth set-up. It did feel like information overload at times but Dick is a tremendously articulate and approachable man with a terrific depth of knowledge. His slides on positional rotation during games helped me a lot and I have adapted some of his drills for my own sessions.

Next we heard from the then UEFA technical director and former Scotland manager Andy Roxburgh on what separates success from failure. This focused on creating a winning mentality among your players. There was also a session on how to incorporate technology into coaching. The software was relatively easy to set up and I put it into practise at Falkirk. I'm very much from the school of thought that a picture is far better than a thousand words. An expert called Ian Donnelly made us aware of a multitude of things that can cloud your judgment when you are simply watching a game. I truly believe video analysis is a valuable tool. Later in the course, we had a Prozone presentation. This is an invaluable aid. I think back to the many times I disagreed with a manager or coach over my responsibilities at any given time. If the video analysis is available there is no hiding place.

Still at Largs we heard from Lars Lagerback, the former

Sweden and Nigeria national coach. His philosophy revolved around creating a strict but respectful environment. He was tough in punishing players for things like lack of punctuality – which is disrespectful to the group – and banning mobile phones, but he would make a point of creating a happy atmosphere and allowing players to express an opinion. I was very impressed with Lars' ethics and agreed with the way he believed in giving the players a lot of responsibility in the way their team should operate.

Although the manager must always make the final decision, I think players appreciate an input. Lars was also very strong on creating a winning culture, whether it be a friendly or a pre-season game, and on players winning their individual battles all over the pitch. Some might see this as giving the coach a get-out for a disappointing performance but, for me, it is more about the empowerment of the individual. Players want belief shown in them by their manager.

Next we had a presentation from a couple of senior referees in Scotland, Euan Norris and Bobby Madden. Both guys came across very well. We were shown a DVD of the match officials' meeting up before a Celtic v Rangers League Cup Final. This gave us an insight into the type of things that are discussed or highlighted. There were also a couple of quizzes, including one on the laws of the game, for which we were split into groups. When it came to assessing actual match situations we got virtually all of our answers correct. But the offside quiz was different. Even on the 'easy' level our group managed to get only 12 out of 20. I think nearly everyone struggles with the offside law – including referees at times! It was certainly helpful to see how difficult the decision-making can be.

The fact that there was a good rapport between the

candidates and the referees made me think about how this seems to be lacking from the game itself. What appears to be missing is the human element and some commonsense. I know the rulebook does not give these guys any grey areas but we saw a human side of them during our discussion which does not rear its head on a Saturday. Going back 10 years or so, you were able to have a bit of banter with the match officials but that has now gone and it is to the detriment of the game in my opinion. This has made the game more difficult for players and referees alike.

It was interesting to hear from former Scotland and Hearts manager Craig Levein about preparing dossiers on the opposition and the preparation of tactics. Craig learned to work the system around the players and not the other way around. You'll perhaps remember how he took a lot of stick for his controversial approach to a European Championship qualifier against the Czech Republic in Prague in 2010. Scotland lined up with a 4-6-0 formation. Yes, Craig admitted, he did set out to get a draw! Scotland lost in the end by the only goal but he explained that he felt a very compact game was needed after analysing the opposition.

Craig knew that in going without a striker he would be at the mercy of the media if he didn't get it right. As such, it was a very brave decision. It wasn't one I would have made but it was enlightening to hear the reasoning behind it, which put a bit of method to the madness. I know Craig relatively well and he's always very honest and up-front. For me, the overriding element is that you must have strength in your convictions. You must trust yourself and be able to learn from the hard times, as Craig did after his fleeting and ill-fated spell in charge of Leicester City. What he did was to write down everything he was feeling in the immediate aftermath of his English experience, then put his notebook away for several weeks and go through it again when he had a clear mind. That shows a willingness to admit to certain mistakes and learn from them.

Fast forward to UEFA headquarters in Switzerland and a course directed by Howard Wilkinson, who impressed me with this quote: 'When you sign a player you get his body. As a top coach, you must get his mind and heart.'

Among course guests was Gareth Southgate, the former England defender who had a spell in charge of Middlesbrough where he admitted he wasn't ready to step up from playing to managing at the tender age of 35. Terry Venables and Martin O'Neill had both turned down the job vacated by Steve McClaren.

Gareth told us: 'In hindsight I didn't really know what questions to ask the chairman. I was naïve and didn't really have a full understanding of the business. I knew I had to have a staff meeting but I wasn't sure how to go about it.'

Despite this, Southgate enjoyed a good relationship with his players. How did he create that trust?

'Always be as honest as you can. I always talked to a player if they were to be dropped. The only time I didn't do it, I had problems and the relationship was never the same again. Also, you have to work with players that are NOT in the team.'

For me, our chat with Gareth was among the highlights of the course. He was someone of our age who had been thrown into a Premier League manager's job. It was a great story that he had done this with very little coaching experience or education. Gareth's honesty on his naivety was very enlightening. The way he described it was exactly the way I think I would have felt in certain situations.

But it also proved to me that I am probably far more

prepared to make the jump into management than I thought. I found myself nodding to the things Gareth talked about, like the chairman not understanding the importance of the assistant manager's role, and the value of talking to players who are being dropped. Gareth sat with us at dinner, continuing to take questions and asking some himself.

There was a session in crisis management and the message I took from this was that, during a bad run, the manager must be more visible, more approachable and more accessible. That is, no hiding and no excuses. Reaction from the public and the media has to be regarded as a distraction and discarded.

Two quotes here from Marcello Lippi: 'When a team plays well the coach takes the credit – when it doesn't, the coach must accept responsibility..

And: 'A coach has to defend his ideas with confidence. Keep cool and calm, even when the pressure is on. Players appreciate coaches like that, it can be highly motivational.'

UEFA media officer Graham Turner contributed to a presentation on the role of television, radio and newspapers in the modern game.

'There is no such thing as off the record!' he said. Doubtless this was advice aimed at post-match situations. He also urged that any controversial incidents be reviewed before doing interviews.

Howard Wilkinson weighed in with a tip often given to politicians, saying 'Don't answer a question unless it's the one you want. Set your own agenda and get your message across.'

One student from each country was chosen to enact a 'flash interview' scenario in front of the television cameras. I was chosen from the SFA group and this was my scenario:

You have just lost at home in the first leg of your Champions League semi-final against Chelsea. Your star midfielder was sent off and you were sent to the stand.

Thanks a lot, nice easy one there! I was given just two minutes thinking time in advance and decided to steer the conversation towards my player being sent off for two yellow cards (less controversial!). Also, I was upbeat, saying the players would be well drilled over the coming week in preparing for the second leg and that my absence from the bench would not affect us. It was important to give everyone a morale boost and lift confidence. Equally, I felt it was important to smile at the right times during the interview to give a sort of knowing look to the tough questioning I was facing.

The media side of things interests me a lot and I'm comfortable with it. I'd like to think I'm good at getting my point across, having done a university degree in Sports Media and Broadcasting. One interesting piece of feedback was Howard Wilkinson's reaction to me saying in the mock interview that I wouldn't be missed on the bench for one 90 minutes. 'You've talked yourself out of your own job,' he said. I can see his point but felt it was more important to empower my staff.

Onwards to the UEFA Under-21 Championships in Denmark – told you that I was busy! Here we heard from England's manager, Stuart Pearce. He reflected on where the team had come from since England finished as runners-up in the previous tournament in Sweden. Stuart pointed out that ten of that original squad were eligible to play again but only five were in the group in Denmark.

He seemed to be indicating here that certain players, and their clubs, had a very poor mentality when it came to the national team at this age group. Pearce, of course, is unfailingly up front and honest. As a player he was highly successful but was always candid about his own failings. Unforgettably, of course, he missed a penalty in England's devastating World Cup semi-final defeat to Germany in 1990. As Under 21 boss, he made sure that his players took part in a penalty shoot-out after EVERY training session! He kept all the conversion stats so that he could work out the best choices for that situation in a tournament.

One thing that struck me was the sense of isolation surrounding the England team in their hotel environment. The FA, or maybe Pearce himself, had felt it necessary to hire out the whole hotel. It was based in a very remote area with no surrounding town within walking distance and no real sense of life. I know the players were there to concentrate on winning but I think they would have liked some other hotel guests around the place to create a bit of atmosphere. It all seemed dead. Yes, young players can be distracted at times but as Pearce himself said, 'You have to give them ownership and responsibility.'

Another personal highlight was hearing a talk on leadership from Gregor Townsend, the former Scottish rugby union player who then became a coach. I genuinely think more collaboration between the two sports could help develop both of them.

One little tip that stood out was among several relayed by Ricky Sbragia, who has been a highly respected coach at Manchester United, Bolton and Sunderland. In the youth set-up at Carrington the coaches never shout instructions to the players.

'This allows us to focus on the game without having to think about instructions to the players. Half-time and full-time are the opportunities to pass on what you have seen,' explained Ricky. I thought of Ricky as a man I would genuinely enjoy working alongside. He just wants to be out there helping players to improve and enjoy the game he loves. His sessions are simple with just the right amount of progression. He loves to see the simple things done well. I really believe he is the kind of guy who would use the saying: Football is a simple game made difficult by the players.

While that is true to an extent, the complexity is in staying fresh enough with your ideas to be one step in front of the opposition. And that, of course, is far from straightforward. It's the very reason for this kind of exhaustive preparation to become a coach. Just ask Andre Villas-Boas who, at the time we met him, was going through a difficult and short-lived reign as manager of Chelsea. AVB, who had become the youngest coach to win a European club title while at Porto, was asked this question by David Unsworth. 'On your first day at Chelsea, what did you say?'

Andre replied: 'I installed a 50" plasma in the dressing room and showed quotes from opposition coaches. I tried to create a revolt, a siege mentality. I also blew up a picture of Manchester United to show where we want to be.'

He said his brief was to reverse Chelsea's downward cycle. 'I only lost three matches at Porto so losing games at Chelsea has been very informative to me. The media try to push you to a confrontation which creates a situation where fans question things at the club. I have been called arrogant recently! I have never been arrogant in my life, but negative, media-driven comments, affect the people around the players which can enter the subconscious.'

AVB also made this valid observation. 'As a manager you have around 25 focal points (the players), they have one (the manager).'

And he was controversial in his views on sports science

and physical testing. I have to say I agree with him that the modern game is completely influenced by science and player statistics to the detriment of the technical and tactical side of the game. Maybe I wouldn't go quite as far as Andre in saying I was not interested but I do feel the sports science guys have far too much influence on training methods, both individually and collectively. It was also great to hear that the first thing he looks for is player intelligence, and that physical height is of no real relevance at all.

I noted down some words that came to mind as AVB spoke … passionate, energetic, determined, stylish, focused, driven, self-belief, honesty, tough. You could say I'm a fan. And I'm delighted to see, as I write this, that Andre is doing some promising things with Spurs.

As if all of this was not riches beyond comprehension for a footballing education, how about a Q and A session with Marcello Lippi? The former Italy player won the Champions League and five Serie A titles as a club manager. He then won the World Cup for his country. In short, one of the all-time great managers.

A few random gems from Lippi … 'Communicate and manage the many personalities for the good of the team … look for intelligent players and create a team with different characters … difficult times create the foundation for your greatest success.'

This is a gentleman who has won everything in the game and yet he spoke with total respect to a group of people he had never met before. Why would he want to come to Scotland to do a question and answer session for the SFA? Because he is a football person. His humility and humour in the way he answered every question (via his interpreter, Manuel Pascali) could only be admired.

The basis of his success, in my opinion, was to create an

environment for a team to evolve. He wanted talent and character while stressing that there was no room for egos in a team dynamic, saying, 'You cannot allow ANYONE to affect the collective.'

Lippi was also very open in admitting to his weaknesses, talking about not coaching further afield as he had never learned another language. Added to this, he allowed for the possibility that his failure at Inter Milan might have had something to do with him trying to mirror the successful ways of Juventus. One great anecdote was how Italy's players had a bet with him at the start of the 2006 World Cup that meant he would have to swim across a lake at the team hotel if they reached the final. It was a fantastic piece of morale-boosting fun … and Italy went on to win the tournament.

Right at the other end of the spectrum came a talk by John McGlynn from my native Scotland. He worked his way up via backroom roles with Hearts to become the inspirational boss of Raith Rovers. In the 2010-11 season John won the PFA Scotland Manager of the Year award. For me, he's the real face of Scottish football. He has honesty and integrity and I can identify with him as he arrived late in the game, having been a plumber by trade.

John wanted to show his players he cared. He cleaned and painted, he bought new training balls, he worked to get a kit deal. In this way he made a positive impression on his players and earned their respect before demanding the same back.

The highs and lows of sport were summed up for us in a very distinctive style by Frank Dick, the former director of coaching of British athletics. Dick – who fronted an era that spawned the likes of Seb Coe, Steve Ovett and Daley Thompson – said there were two types of people in life.

These were:

- VALLEY PEOPLE: Woulda-shoulda-coulda type people.
- MOUNTAIN PEOPLE: Those who take the risk of winning and for whom change is opportunity.

Another of Frank's sayings was this: 'There is no certainty in life, only uncertainty. Use that uncertainty and turn it to your advantage. If you see a team-mate having a tough time on the pitch, it's not HIS problem, it's the TEAM'S problem.'

Besides a study visit to a foreign club (I went to Club Desportivo Nacional of Portugal), we spent a highly illuminating day with Everton. When you think of Everton you think automatically of David Moyes … or at least you did until he became the successor to Sir Alex's throne at Manchester United. At Goodison, David created a fantastic working environment for ALL employees of the club and it was built on one word: Respect. Not so much respect for him as manager but respect for the club as a whole. From the minute we arrived at the training ground we were treated like royalty. There was no 'them and us' feel about it. This was 'one for all and all for one.' The first team players spoke to the ground-staff and cleaners in the same tone as they would the manager or chairman.

David Moyes the man – according to former charges Alan Stubbs, Davy Weir and David Unsworth – is a footballing maniac. In the nicest possible way, of course. He would study video footage over and over again, constantly asking questions of his staff and himself. Apparently Moyes would beat himself up for days if he felt after a defeat or draw that his players were not given the information they required for a match.

Everton has had to live in the shadow of a more illustrious neighbour over the years but in recent times the pendulum has swung. I believe this comes down to a togetherness that many football clubs fail to achieve. I was pleased to see Moyes take over from Fergie. He deserved the job in my opinion. Success is relative. David may not have won a trophy in his 11 years at Everton but, in budgetary terms, he had them punching above their weight almost throughout his time there. A club can realistically ask for no more than that.

Although Manchester United didn't appoint from within when the great man finally stood down – as Liverpool did during the famous 'boot room' days – there is a similar feeling about the way continuity is being maintained at Old Trafford.

It would have jarred if Fergie had just left altogether rather than becoming a director and the club had brought in, say, a totally different type of personality from outside. No matter how successful that individual may have been in the past, they could well have struggled. Manchester United is more than a club, it is a culture. Some call it a brand and, much as I'm suspicious of that word, it does apply in that there is something truly distinctive about the place. All thanks to Fergie.

Beyond being a Scot, Moyes shares some of the same characteristics. He has similar intensity to Sir Alex and an equally driven nature. Maybe Alex saw something of himself in the former Everton boss? I glimpsed a bit of that in the way Moyes made Everton an all-embracing institution. The whole club mattered to him. The place had a sense of identity and Moyes' presence was stamped all over it. You feel Sir Alex will have liked that.

One more thing while we're on this subject. People ask me why it is that so many of us Scots do well in management. Maybe it's down to the working class background in the majority of cases. It's also been said, and perhaps with a degree of truth, that the Scottish accent sounds quite aggressive and authoritative. We normally get right to the point. And we can make people jump!

Preparing for management also involves taking a peek over the other side of the fence. You might not like the view but it's important to understand the workings of the football boardroom. There is no single typical example because chairmen can be very different. Their decisions are often personality-led and in the case of some of the more recent foreign owners it's very hard to work out their rationale. But the Pro Licence quite rightly involves seeing the game from their perspective. You may not be overly familiar with the name of Rod Petrie but he was the perfect guy to hear from, having overseen – at the time of our meeting – the hiring and firing of 12 managers in Scotland! This was across his then 16 years with Hibernian where he has variously held the roles of managing director, chief executive and chairman.

Petrie comes from a financial and business background having worked for accountants Ernst & Young and merchant bankers Quayle Munro plc. He stressed to us that the relationship between chairman and manager must be strong to have any kind of success. We were shown a must-do list for each person in the relationship and the top two of five points were the same for both:

- Trust
- Communicate

The other three must-dos for the chairman were:

- Allow you (the manager) to do your job
- Protect
- Motivate

And for the manager:

- Do your job
- Do what you say
- Win!

Note the all-important three-letter word at the bottom. Last but by no means least, you might say.

Rod Petrie's definition of the two roles was summed up thus. 'You manage the players and I'll manage the contracts.' He saw his main function as to handle the budget.

As for the process of appointing a manager, one thing a club like Hibs never has to do is to advertise. Over 100 genuine applicants would be the norm and, unlike some clubs in this age of lack of communication and common courtesy, they would all receive a reply for good or bad. Petrie would then formulate a short list with the other directors and begin interviewing. This used to be just a one-to-one conversation. Now it's a wide-ranging process with the modern manager using PowerPoint and DVDs to support his credentials and philosophy.

This is what Petrie's board would look for:

- UEFA Pro Licence
- Winning track record
- Playing style/ tactics
- Development of young players

- Discipline
- International standard

Among qualities demanded by Petrie would be someone who is motivational, inspirational and respectful. He would also need to have a good media presence and be able to build up good relationships with all staff.

Finally, these are Petrie's golden rules for himself:

- Leave the dressing room to the manager
- Only sign players the manager has seen with his own eyes
- Support the manager to do what he does best
- Make sure the manager has a good assistant

And this last one is an absolute pearler. Petrie's last golden rule to himself:

- Any player recommendation from the chairman should be dismissed!

Not every chairman/owner has that kind of humility and willingness to laugh at his own expense. Too many think they know better than the manager when it comes to football. I thought Mr. Petrie spoke very well, portraying both himself and his football club in a positive light. In his time at Easter Road they have rarely lost money, consistently produced high quality young players and upgraded both the stadium and the training facilities.

BUT ... I have to say 12 managers in 16 years is an horrendous record. There is no getting away from that in my book, much as I formed some admiration for the man and was certainly grateful, as were we all, for his input.

'Ruthless' is a word often associated with Rod Petrie and I was left feeling uncertain as to whether we had seen the real man on show. Was there more being kept back? Whatever, it was an invaluable learning experience. As was the course as a whole.

22

Who'd be a Manager?
Who Wouldn't?

It strikes me you can guarantee two things about the job that football managers do. One is that they will get sacked. The other is that there will always be a big queue to take their places. In between there will be much hand-wringing. People will be condemning the madness of it all. Some will claim that nobody will want to work for this club or that club, this chairman or that chairman. But all the while the phone calls, emails and texts will flood in to that club and that chairman. Usually they are spoilt for choice. It's simply because the casualty rate is so high that there are as many, if not more, managers and coaches outside the game than those working in it. There is always far more supply than demand.

It also means that you will find managers being prepared to work at a level their careers have far exceeded. Here's a couple of examples. Kevin Blackwell led two prestigious Championship clubs to within one game of the Premier League. He was unlucky enough to lose play-off finals with both Leeds United and Sheffield United, having also coached the Blades' team that fell at the last hurdle under Neil Warnock a few years earlier.

Despite his apparently excellent record, Kevin was out of the game for more than two years after being dismissed from Bramall Lane only a couple of games into the 2010-11 season. There was widespread sympathy but the game is harsh. Blackwell was shelved all of a sudden. And when he returned it was with Bury at the bottom of League One and irreversibly on their way down to the basement.

Then there is the case of my old Wednesday boss Brian Laws. We didn't always see eye to eye but he did well to last three years at Hillsborough considering the financial constraints of that era. That was recognised by Burnley when they were in the Premier League and Brian suddenly had a shot at top flight management. Burnley were relegated, as was always likely in any case. Brian had them in play-off contention midway through the following season only for the axe to fall. When he got back into the game it was also with a team struggling in League One as he began another spell at Scunthorpe where he succeeded in his formative years as a manager but, like Blackwell at Bury, could not stave off relegation.

This is not a cry for sympathy. I doubt whether any of the guys who go in for these jobs would want any. They know the rules. They are there to be shot at. Does it put me off? No, not at all, because I would be going in with my eyes wide open. I saw enough managers come and go in my playing career to know that there is no security in that job. I suppose it's part of the excitement to dodge the bullets. A sort of Russian roulette.

The stakes are high but then so are the rewards for success and football management is a pretty well paid occupation when all's said and done. Nobody drags anybody kicking and screaming into it. As I say, they are queueing up out of the door and down the street for almost any job at any level.

171

But it doesn't mean that the huge upheaval is necessarily right. Far from it. Some of the decisions beggar belief. There were a couple of sackings during the 2012-13 season that had everyone in and around the game absolutely gobsmacked.

Sean O'Driscoll was just settling in as Nottingham Forest manager with a team pushing for the play-offs when he was thrown out within hours of a 4-2 home win over Leeds.

Even harsher was the case of Nigel Adkins at Southampton. This guy had performed a miracle. He'd won successive promotions from League One to put the Saints back in the big time. After a sticky start they were actually above the relegation places, more than par for the course in my book, when he was asked to leave. Astonishing.

The common denominator is that Forest and Southampton were in foreign ownership. That was also the case at Blackburn where a number of equally strange decisions were being made around that time. They sacked three managers within the season and, all told, had five guys in charge of the team.

It's natural, I suppose, for people who buy clubs to want to call the shots. They have paid handsomely for the privilege. But it seems their hearts rule their heads when it comes to football. It's as if they reject a lot of the principles that made them successful in business. Delegation is the way of the commercial world. The boss of a chemicals firm isn't necessarily a whizz with a test tube. The manager of a rail company won't be found driving a train. Yet when it comes to football everybody thinks they are an expert. How much better would some foreign owners, not all, fare if they took proper advice?

I say 'not all' because the chairman who came to the rescue of Sheffield Wednesday, Milan Mandaric, is not only very passionate about the game but also very knowledgeable.

He was steeped in it before he even entered football in this country. For others, it is a totally new environment. They would be doing themselves a huge favour if they recognised their limitations accordingly.

That said, the game can never be run completely as a business. Balance sheets are cold and clinical. Profits are a cause for celebration but only by those at the top and the shareholders. There is no dancing in the street. Football supporters don't measure success or failure in financial terms. Not in the slightest. Rightly or wrongly – probably the latter – they'd rather win a trophy or promotion and go into debt than rock up in mid-table and break even. That's the difference. As football's 'shareholders' they have more of an emotional investment than a financial one, even if it's a costly business following your club these days.

What sort of a price do you put on fulfilling dreams? How can you quantify it? You can't. It's why clubs will overstretch to realise those dreams, why owners will spend beyond reasonable means to be seen as the good guy who delivered rather than a tight-fisted killjoy. Football is a lot about ego.

I was interested to read a Sheffield Telegraph interview with Milan Mandaric, who told my co-author last season: 'You see some owners just put the money in and let somebody else run the business. You can't correct everything with money. You've got to have presence, skill and experience – and surround yourself with the right people. Whether it's playing with money or ego or whatever, I see some owners who don't participate with the club and the emotions of the club, which is what makes football a great business. You need to operate from the heart and the head. One is no good without the other.'

I should add, though, that supporters have become far

more understanding of the business side. It has been a rude awakening considering the number of clubs who have plunged into crisis. To keep their followers onside, clubs also have to be a bit more honest about the financial realities rather than promising dreams they can't fulfil. More openness leads to greater awareness of what can and can't be done. Not that there still isn't scope for achievement against the odds. Bradford City reaching the League Cup Final in 2013? Who on earth could have predicted that?

As for the so-called managerial merry-go-round, there are times when we are guilty of over-analysing it. Sometimes it is beyond any logical explanation. That can be equally true about events on the field and I suppose the off-field stuff just reflects that. Where it has gone slightly out of kilter, though, is in the influence held by supporters. Of course, they have always had their say. In the old days their say was simply shouted from the terraces or stands. Players, manager and directors listened but the fans were 'out of their ear' once the game was over.

Now that voice of protest is deafening. It can be heard for every minute of every day until the team next takes to the field. Fans have more ammunition than just letters to newspapers and calls to phone-ins. There's Twitter and fans' forums. It's a drip-drip effect that can lead to a torrent. Managers are swept away by this great force of public opinion which can magnify a couple of defeats into a crisis. Boards listen to this cacophany of sound before sacking managers and appointing new ones. It's easy to say they shouldn't, that they should block it out and think for themselves. But there's just no escaping the beast of the social media.

So it follows that the job of manager is more difficult and demanding than ever before. Most of them can't really build a squad over time and plan for the future. What future? They have to work for today and hope that tomorrow takes care of itself. It's not healthy for the game and not conducive, either, to the development of youngsters when clubs are having to go for the short-term option of taking an experienced player on loan rather than promoting one of the kids. But this is the reality and we either accept it or we don't. Once the football bug bites it won't let go. Who'd be a manager? When the time is right, I know I would!

23

Fast-Tracking the Kids ... but I Never Was a Slow Coach!

Warning! There's going to be a fair bit of terminology in this chapter. Now I'm a fairly plain and straightforward fella. I try to see things as they are and tell them as they are. Football, as many of the great managers have pointed out, is essentially a simple game. But you saw in the previous chapter just how much stuff managers have to get their head around these days. And there's no doubt the game is becoming ever more scientific. Some of it might be good, some of it might be bad. You decide. But the fact is that you have to work within the system if you want a career in the game and another reality is that nothing in life ever stands still. Reasonably fresh from playing, I'm in a better position to move with the times than some of those coaches and managers who have been in the game a long time.

The Elite Player Performance Plan. There, what did I tell you? This was the framework for my first coaching job in England as I stepped into a role back at Sheffield Wednesday in the summer of 2012. Sean McAuley came through for me and I was able to combine a position back at Hillsborough with helping Nicola on the estate agency business. The EPPP resulted from the flow of foreigners into our game and the need to increase the number of home-grown players gaining professional contracts. It was also aimed at creating more coaching time for young players and measuring their progress more accurately.

As such, the FA and Premier League felt there had to be more documentation on what coaches and players were doing on a day-to-day basis. In effect, a monitoring exercise. At this point I'll have to hit you with something else, a book called *Bounce*. Ever heard of it? For those who haven't, it was written by former table tennis champion Matthew Syed and sub-titled: *The myth of talent and the power of practice.*

Syed's theory is that it takes 10,000 hours of practice across 10 years to achieve elite performance level. Football has largely adopted the principle. All players are encouraged to work towards the 10,000 hours on the basis that, by the time the target is clocked up, they will be at their peak around the age of 28.

From under-10s upwards, the hours of all kids associated with professional clubs are being monitored and recorded. It's no different for those nine or ten years older, the age group I'm dealing with on a day-to-day basis. These are what we call the development players. I'm open-minded, as I say, but there is a negative side to this. The danger is that you can be spending more time on the computer than on the training ground. It's become a bit like the way education is heading. Speak to any group of teachers and many will tell you that they are so engulfed by paperwork that they barely have time to teach. Or that it becomes the least of their priorities when it should be the most important. Believe it or not, football coaching is going a bit like that. Potentially, it is going too far in that academic direction.

Every one of our sessions has to be accounted for. Then again, I don't necessarily think it's a bad thing. Time will tell, as they say. We have to embrace modern thinking along with the old school mentalities in the game. People are trying to find reasons why, for instance, England's national team is not performing in major tournaments. Against that, you have to say there was no monitoring of coaching in 1966. Mind you, in those days players would smoke like troopers, drink eight pints the night before a game and eat steak and chips as a pre-match meal. So new thinking is often for the better. You just have to take the best out of it and throw away the worst. When it comes to monitoring you hope there will be a balance somewhere along the way.

The theorists are trying to tell us that natural talent is a myth and that achievement is all a product of practice. But every so often a George Best will come along and blind you with the gift of natural brilliance. Try coaching someone like him. There are many other examples of players who could be taught very little when it comes to technique because they had it all by birth and had worked out the rest for themselves. Unfortunately, I haven't come across one yet! Here's hoping ...

The bottom line is that anything is good if it's successful. Remember how Paul Sturrock had us drinking wine and vodka at the training ground before our vital league game at Hull in 2005. If you win, as we did, then it's great management. But if you lose then it's considered crazy. Brian Clough famously adopted similar 'relaxation' techniques before big games at Nottingham Forest. Granted, that was in a different era altogether. But there will still be managers today who will consider loosening up their players in such a fashion. The trick is to make sure nobody finds out if it doesn't work!

I love my job at Wednesday. It's immensely enjoyable. So much so that I haven't thought twice about staying when there has been talk of me moving on. For instance, I was linked with a couple of jobs in March this year. As I mentioned previously, Steven Pressley moved from Falkirk, where we had formed a strong partnership, to Coventry City for his first management job in England. Steven had been in the market for that sort of opportunity for a while and I was delighted for him.

He took over the Sky Blues in difficult circumstances with the club in League One. But that's the sort of challenge which commonly presents itself these days and I hope it works out for Steven. There is the potential for him to further his reputation with a club of great tradition and a relatively high profile. Equally, there were rumours that I might replace him at Falkirk where a lot of the fans were calling for me. But again, while flattered, my family circumstances had changed and I'd become committed to a working life in England revolving around my Sheffield base.

Development squad coaches are a little below the general media radar so let me explain my role. I'm responsible for a group of around seven first-year pros who occasionally get supplemented by players on trial and the best of the Under-18s. Dean Ramsdale, a very respected guy who worked previously for Burnley and Preston, heads up our academy operation following Sean McAuley's departure for an opportunity in America's MLS.

I operate alongside another experienced coach in Neil Thompson, who formerly worked on the youth side at Leeds, and Max Wragg, a recent young professional at Wednesday who had the misfortune to be released. Max's input is invaluable and I don't think he realises just how much he helps the kids in the respect that they are much closer to his age than the rest of us.

It has to be said that Sheffield Wednesday are four or five

years behind the majority of clubs at the same level when it comes to developing young players. That's purely because of our unfortunate recent history, the familiar background of financial problems and the issue of ownership which was finally resolved when Milan Mandaric took over, saving the Owls from the imminent certainty of going into administration.

This is no criticism of previous boards who had a hard job just keeping the place afloat. The priority had to be the first team over the academy. Obviously the same has to be true now to a certain extent and, as I write this, we are facing a battle to stay in the Championship. But the chairman and manager, Dave Jones, are empowering the academy staff to push on and improve the youth side, whereas in the past Sean probably felt he had one arm tied behind his back.

There is a comparison I can't avoid because it's well documented that Sheffield United have produced a lot of very good players in recent times. We are talking about talents such as Phil Jagielka, Kyle Walker, Kyle Naughton and Matthew Lowton. It hasn't necessarily improved the team's performance, apart from one season in the Premier League a few years ago, but some big fees have been raised to help with the finances at Bramall Lane.

I can't think of a single comparable player produced by Wednesday in my time around the club and the dearth of young talent goes back a lot further than that. Where does this have its roots? Well, I suppose you could speculate that nobody was looking at young talent during the club's last successful era in the 1990s when Wednesday won the League Cup and got into Europe. That success could not be sustained and now we are starting at base in looking to the longer term. As I speak, we don't have a single lad in the Under 21 group who's come all the way through the

Sheffield Wednesday system.

We play in a league and when it comes to games we have to make sure we are not over-burdening young players. It's between the ages of 17 and 21 that they have growth spurts, which have to be borne in mind. We're allowed to use three over-age players in matches, essentially first-teamers who are on the fringe of the side or ones who need a game after coming back from injury. What we have to do is provide a quick progression through the junior ranks. If players are good enough they are old enough and will be given opportunities. There are a couple of 15-year-olds who, at the time of writing, are attracting the attention of the big clubs.

There's some really good inter-action between the first team set-up and ours. Dave Jones has been terrific at integrating the two. For example, some of our kids get the experience of training with the first team and vice versa. Yes, we'll have the odd first-teamer training with us. What better way to learn than by example? And, of course, when the kids get to train with the seniors they work their whatsits off to prove themselves and maybe catch the eye of the manager.

At the end of the season there'll be the usual release-and-recruit mechanism. It's the cruel side of football but it has to be done. Supporters never see this aspect of the game and it's perhaps just as well. Whereas high profile players have to swallow their bad news in public, at least the kids get the knock-backs in private. Not that they hurt any the less. We have to rely on their parents to pick up the pieces. But I feel I have an important role to play here because I'm the perfect guy to tell any kid we release that it might not be the end of the world. I can say: Look at me. I was told I wasn't good enough at three clubs in Scotland – Stenhousemuir,

Meadowbank and Dunfermline – and I still made a decent career out of the game. What's more, I did so without anywhere near the practice hours now demanded because I was part-time and had a 'proper' job. Now throw in the fact that I wasn't blessed, shall we say, with outstanding natural ability and you can see what can be achieved through dedication and determination.

Our planning for the end of the last season was that we would keep four and release three. Yes, it's that harsh but then it has to be. Space has to be created for those pushing from below and as we speak there are five earmarked to step up from the Under 18s into the development squad. I'm in every day apart from Sundays and Wednesdays. The lads will do double sessions two or three times a week. It's ball work, technique and tactics in the mornings with the physical stuff in the afternoons. The lads train for a lot longer than the first-teamers but then they need to. Their match commitments are fewer, only 22 league games compared to 46 plus the cups for the seniors. The training is geared to make them stronger, fitter and more flexible. Along the way they'll have the chance to take part in behind-closed-doors friendlies arranged by the manager. This is to get them used to a more physical game with a higher tempo.

A criticism often made of most clubs these days, and a justifiable one, is that as soon as they have a problem position to fill in the first team they go out and bring someone in on loan rather than blood a youngster. While there is all this talk about windows, in reality the market for loans is hardly ever closed. It means you get players darting around all over the place. Managers are often looking for a ready-made replacement for a player they have lost, ideally someone with experience. Or, if that's not possible, then an up-and-coming player from the Premiership whose club are looking to loan him out for match action.

A team's league position will dictate how they use the loan system. If they are pushing for promotion or fighting relegation then there's an obvious tendency to borrow what you need. That said, three points for a win has meant there are very few sides with nothing to play for even in the closing weeks of a season. So there is a natural concern across the board about whether there really is a proper outlet for the investment in the academy system. Besides, you never really know if a youngster is good enough unless you stick him in the first team. It can be sink or swim for the kid – but then that could also be true for the team.

You can see the dilemma and conflict of interest here. Certainly, you'd be very brave to throw a kid into a relegation battle. All I can say is that at Wednesday last season we had a manager who, if the youngster was good enough, would have had the courage to do it. Dave Jones threw Aaron Ramsey into a promotion-chasing team at Cardiff. I know he would also have done it if the side had been near the bottom. Ramsey's subsequent development with Arsenal has more than justified that gamble.

Would I like to see a clampdown on the loan system? Maybe a ruling that you can't loan players for most of the season? As a youth coach, my answer would be YES. But if I was a manager whose job depended on going up or surviving relegation then my response would be an emphatic NO. Besides, there is such great pressure from fans to bring in players. Of course, there is an element of risk as with any recruitment. Paul Sturrock made an inspired move when he loaned Kenwyne Jones from Southampton during our promotion season. Equally, Paul would admit that taking Gabby Agbonlahor from Aston Villa did not work out. The lad was brought in to play wide and, while talented, he didn't cut it. He went back to Villa and emerged as a goalscoring striker. That made our fans wonder why Paul barely used him. It can cut both ways.

On the flip side, Scott Carson was an outstanding loan goalkeeper whereas Brad Jones wasn't. But Brad went on to make it big with a move to Liverpool. Who'd be a manager? But where loans will always be popular is that you can quickly correct a mistake on a loan player by sending him back, which you can't do with a full transfer.

Of course, I see a difference in kids from my era but then I'm bound to as my own development was so very different. My upbringing saw me eventually come through as a late developer. Nowadays a lot of the kids want to run before they can walk. I find that frustrating as someone who had to work for success and appreciated it all the more when it came. The expectations some of them have now makes it all the harder for them if they are released between the ages of 18 and 21. Where do they go from there?

One kid we released last season, Cecil Nyoni, went into non-league. Will he ever have the opportunity to get back? I'm generalising here but sometimes young players don't realise the opportunity they have until it's gone. They can't always be led by the coach. They have to show the drive and motivation to succeed on their own behalf, like coming back to put in those extra hours on the training ground. Being dedicated can make all the difference. Besides football, youngsters go on education programmes. Some of them disregard this completely which is foolish in the extreme considering the uncertainties ahead.

One thing where I've had to step in – and where I think I can help the lads – is in the way they use the social media. It's a funny old world at the moment. There's more communication between people than ever before, more 'chatting' if you like, and yet a lot less actual conversation. Sometimes it's as if nobody speaks to each other anymore. People text each other when they could be in adjoining rooms of the same office or house even. Millions of emails are chasing each other around the globe and it seems people are reluctant to use the telephone. Walk down the street and folk have their heads down. Even on the move, they can text or tweet, or check for messages. No-one has eyes for the world around them.

Now let me tell you here and now that I'm no stick in the mud when it comes to using modern technology and the social media. Some of the above certainly applies to me as well. The iPhone is an addictive device, I have to admit. It's more than just a business or social tool. You have the whole world at your fingertips. It takes a strong will not to keep running through the various programmes. There's sweat on the brow that you might have missed a message while you are filling up the car with petrol! Above all, a smart phone is both a business and a leisure tool. That's what makes it so difficult to switch off – in every sense of the phrase!

All of this explains why one of my early decisions as a youth coach at Hillsborough was to ban mobiles and personal headphones from the dressing room. Before I did that, nobody was talking to anybody. There was no communication. All the lads were sitting quietly in corners of the room. You can't be having that. In football, you need a lively atmosphere. You need chat and banter. Okay, I do allow a ghetto blaster, but that often provokes a response even if it's 'that's a load of crap, get it off.'

And so we come to Twitter. Here again I have to declare an interest because I absolutely love it. As we speak, I'm lucky enough to have nearly 10,000 followers. For all the downside of getting occasional abuse from idiots, trolls as they call them, Twitter is actually a very warm place.

There are a lot of lovely, genuine people out there who use it in just the right way. They don't always agree with an opinion you might have but then why should they? Providing the 'argument' is in the right spirit, it's just knockabout fun. And of course, as we are always being told, football is a game of opinions. Quite right, too.

From my journeyman career, I'm fortunate to have picked up followers from a number of clubs, many of whom have expressed an interest in this book. It's in that way that Twitter can be a business tool as well, as it is for the estate agency. But when it comes to the business of football you have to be very careful. Different rules apply. The game is an inferno of viewpoints, intrigue and gossip. Information dripped out from the inside only fuels the fire, and it can severely burn the person responsible. That's why, at the time I came to starting this memoir, you couldn't find a single professional football manager on Twitter. But as for the players, tell me one who wasn't on it!

Here, then, is the nub of the problem. The players tweet and their bosses don't. No wonder there's conflict. That said, when I last looked there were, to my surprise, five in-work managers on Twitter, although they seemed to use it to put out information only, not to debate with supporters. Most famously of all, there was Edgar Davids tweeting at Barnet in a Twitter line-up that included Neil Lennon (Celtic), Lee Johnson (Oldham) and Wayne Burnett (Dagenham and Redbridge). The fifth name, Ronnie Moore of Tranmere, was the most surprising of all in that he is an old-school manager. Then I noted that Ronnie had deleted his account after being sent a death-wish by one supposed supporter. How sickening is that! I was even moved to tweet at the time to say this highlighted why Twitter wasn't for managers.

At Sheffield Wednesday, as at many other clubs, we've had a number of incidents of players talking out of turn. Dave Jones has referred, on more than one occasion, to Twitter being the scourge of football. His frustration is justified and easily understandable. For whatever reason, some players think it's okay to swear, kick out or divulge private information on Twitter; stuff they might not say anywhere else.

Naturally, most of the lads I coach are on it. Here I have an advantage over managers. They can't be on Twitter whereas I can. That is to say, I am far enough below the radar to be on it. Would I use Twitter if and when I became a manager? Well, yes and no. I would use it as an ear rather than a voice. I'd monitor what was being said but I wouldn't tweet, or at least certainly not about my club. Doing that would only open me up to all sorts of reaction from the supporters.

You can't be getting involved with that, the job is hard enough. That's not to say I wouldn't communicate properly via the media or go on a fans forum or a radio phone-in. But there's no way you can live with the drip, drip of opinions round the clock every minute of the day. And all night, for that matter. It would drive you mad to listen to it all and perhaps feel you had to respond.

It's different for me now. I'm a sort of Twitter policeman when it comes to the kids at the training ground. I follow them all. And if they tweet something that's out of order then I will tell them – on Twitter! For example, if one of them is swearing I'll quote their tweet and put something on the end like: 'Language? No need!' It tends to pull them up short. Getting a ticking off like that in front of their mates can be more effective than a face-to-face rollocking.

But, of course, I tell them as well how not to use Twitter. It should be common sense but, as I say, people generally, not just footballers, have this idea you can say anything you like on there. You can't. It's a public forum and these lads, because of the nature of their job, have thousands of followers. They have to be careful. I've seen kids get sacked because of things they've put out, racist stuff and the like.

They're aware of the guidelines and they all have to sign up to an agreement on usage of the social media. My message is that they should never put out anything that they wouldn't say on the club's website. I tell them to think and take a deep breath before hitting that 'tweet' button. Read it again. Would you say that in a newspaper? You tell them once, you tell them twice and yet occasionally they still get it wrong. Effing and blinding in public is just plain wrong.

The lads have to understand they are responsible to themselves and their family. When I pull them up on Twitter they normally come back and say 'you're right.' They do realise afterwards. Replying to them in public is my way of saying I could be a supporter out there responding to what they've just said. In fairness, they've got a lot better at it.

How do I define success in my job? A good question and one I ask myself. My first conclusion is that if my Under-21s are top of the league then I'm not doing my job right! To do that I might have to hold back my best players from getting first team experience or going out on loan … for the sake of me getting my hands on a trophy at that level. No way is that right for me, the club or the boys themselves. Success in my role is producing players. Full stop.

I have three aims when I go about the job and they are:

- Pushing players into the first team squad
- Getting players noticed enough to go out on loan for senior experience

- Attracting the attention of big club scouts

The third of those might not be welcome if there is a risk of losing a player but it does show that I am doing my job right if it happens. And it has already. I had a couple of lads at the time of writing – an attacking midfielder and a right back – who were being looked at by the likes of Manchester United, Manchester City and Arsenal. I try to keep them out of the spotlight as far as possible at this embryo stage. Careers can blossom and then fizzle out in the teenage years. Players are still developing physically and so many things, including the obvious distractions of youth, can go wrong. But talent is talent and if you can nurture it properly then you will have people looking.

What happens after that isn't really my responsibility but it is an immensely frustrating part of the game that a club can groom a player and then have him spirited away by one of the big clubs. Often there is a pittance paid in compensation. And don't forget the big clubs are out there looking for these gems when the boys are as young as 13 or 14. You'd expect me to say it's unfair but then it so obviously isn't right. I want our best products to play for our first team.

Having said that, if we can produce players that make good business to sell for substantial fees then we are doing something right as well. But that usually only happens when they are in your first team making a reputation for themselves. We have to try doing everything possible to ensure the situation develops that far.

We had one major disappointment, not least for me personally, just as this book was being put to bed. It made headlines in the local press that one of our best kids, Hayden White, turned down the pro contract we offered and chose to join Bolton Wanderers instead. One of the upsetting things for me was that I'd made the decision to convert Hayden from a right winger into a right back. He had a lot to learn defensively but it was in that position that he started to shine and earn himself a long list of admirers.

If a Premier League club comes in for a youngster then you can't do much other than hold your hands up. Maybe Bolton are slightly better placed than us, having finished just outside the play-offs last season, but the bottom line is that they are still a Championship club, so that's a cause for frustration. That said, Hayden had never actually agreed to sign for us. I don't think it was a financial consideration for him. My feeling is that he was simply persuaded he was better off going elsewhere. Whether it was the right decision, time will tell.

But rather than dwell on what we don't have I reckon it's better to highlight what we do have. Several other youngsters did sign pro forms for us at the end of last season. They were defenders Johnny Fenwick and Ayo Obileye plus striker Emmanuel Dieseruvive and goalkeeper Cameron Dawson. Another of our graduates, Adam Hinchliffe, was also offered a pro contract. We had four of them signed up at the time of writing and that's a great return. But I'm greedy. I'd like it to have been five, six or seven.

The lads concerned are not ready for first-team football as yet, although at their age things can change – for better or for worse – within a matter of months. It's the manager who has the final decision on whether to put them on professional terms. Cameron, the keeper, is one in whom we have high hopes. He has a three-year deal with us, having already represented England at Under 18 and 19 level. When did we last have a young player doing that at Sheffield Wednesday? Looking at the others, Obileye has had clubs like Arsenal taking a peek at him.

All in all, it's been a very successful year and hugely satisfying. Moving players forward to take on the next challenge is what the development squad is all about. We have to take it as a compliment, a pat on the back if you like, if other clubs want to sign them. Hopefully we get to keep most of them and then reap the benefits as a club further down the line.

As for loans, they can work for both the club and the player. Caolan Lavery is one bright spark who had a relatively successful loan spell with Paul Sturrock at Southend last season. Another, Matt Fletcher, did a stint with Cambridge. Our whole operation is geared towards pushing the best boys through as quickly as possible. If a youngster is going great guns with the Under 18s, don't keep him there. Let's have him in the development squad. Which is why we sadly have to move players on. I coach right across the board. One day a week we'll have the 18s and 21s together in one big group. Then we'll split them up to work separately with defenders, midfielders and strikers. I remember how John Blackley was specifically a defensive coach and I took a lot from that.

As for my thoughts on how the game should be played, well I favour a passing style. But I do believe in being flexible. The game is evolving all the time and we are moving much more towards a possession game. That means you need composure on the ball from every player, including your defenders. Come to that, your goalkeeper also has to be good with the ball at his feet. The back-pass law has changed the game in that respect, meaning that keepers often have to get themselves out of tight corners where they are not allowed to handle the ball.

For all these reasons I like to work in smaller areas. In passing drills you are looking for players to be comfortable on the ball with opponents all around them. It can be achieved with repetition and a bit of variety thrown in. Players have to feel confident in the drills they are doing. The big word for me is trust. They have to trust themselves to take the ball, and trust the player they pass it to.

A passing game is the ideal but you must always have a Plan B. Inevitably, there will be times when you come up against a team that is better than you. Why? Simply because they have better players. But that need not mean that they are collectively better or more effective on the day. You have to adapt your game accordingly. Remember how Chelsea beat Barcelona in the Champions League last season. It can happen. Another example from closer experience was the way Wednesday accounted for Premier League Fulham in the Capital One Cup in 2012. Dave Jones came out with a memorable phrase afterwards. He said, 'We set our traps.' That's exactly what he did and Fulham fell into them. Wednesday backed off, let Fulham have the ball and hit them on the counter-attack. None of this is exactly new but it does go to show that there will always be ways to win with inferior players.

Dave Jones, Stuart Gray and the senior management team have been great with me. There's trust between us and they allow plenty of interaction with the first team. Sometimes I'll have six or seven senior players mixing in with the youngsters for a practice game and Dave will let me take it. As for my coaching technique, it's very much do as I say and not as I do … I'm often preaching everything I couldn't do as a player! But if I get any backchat I just reach for 'that goal' on YouTube. It's one I scored for Dunfermline against Hearts, the best of my career and I like to think that any striker in the world would have been proud of it. Take a look and clock the fact that it really is me!

24

Coming up Short … I Wanted to Call This 'Around the World in 80 Clubs!'

Well, I certainly achieved the 'round the world' bit. You could say it was only the number of times the world went round the sun that beat me on the other. In 20 years I played for 14 club teams. It sometimes escapes the football historians that I turned out on a few occasions for an outfit called Kitchee early in my time in Hong Kong.

I get asked pretty much the same question all athletes get asked when their active days are over. And I get asked it a lot. 'Would you change anything about your career?'

I suppose I get asked it more than most because I've taken so many twists and turns, so many changes of direction. Some say, 'Don't you wish you had reached the top as a player and made it at Premier League level?'

Well, yes, you've got me there. Of course I do. It's the one and only thing I'd like to change. But it could only have been achieved if I'd been good enough, which I wasn't. But just supposing I had made it in a big way. Even then, I wouldn't have seen the places and met the people I came across in my footballing journey of some 24,000 miles. They do say I've got some miles on the clock. They'd be right there! You can't put a price on spending time in Australia, Hong Kong and Greece, plus the experience of tournament visits to Vietnam and Taiwan. And what about the fact that I've played against England – without even being an international player myself?

Naturally I have a few souvenirs and pride of place goes to my shirt collection. My prize exhibits include the shirts off the back of the great former France and Chelsea defender Frank Leboeuf, and ex-England captain Tony Adams, who I cornered after the Hong Kong friendly. I also tried for the shirts of a couple of former Sheffield Wednesday stars, although I had no affinity with the Owls at the time. One of those belonged to Dejan Stefanovic and the other to Roland Nilsson. I succeeded with Stefanovic but failed narrowly with Nilsson. Somebody beat me to it in the case of the classy Swede who was a player I always admired and was an absolute legend at Hillsborough around the peak of his career.

What else wouldn't I have done if I'd been a big-timer? Well, I'd never have been on a surf board and ridden the waves rolling in to the golden sands of Australia. And I'd never have met some amazing characters. One was a lad from New Zealand who lived with me for a time in my flat on the outskirts of Sydney. He was looking for a place and I had a spare room. When he moved in he turned up with a rucksack, three surf boards … and a black widow spider! It wasn't what I wanted to see, shall we say. There it was, this highly venomous creature which has a bite that can be fatal. Its owner kept it in a clear Perspex box. He looked after it and fed it. I'm not sure the spider ever came out of that box. If it did, I didn't see it! But every morning I'd get up and check that it was still in there. Why did I ever allow that scenario to unfold? Curiosity, I suppose.

I'm also reminded to look back to my early days with hometown Penicuik Athletic. What jogged my memory was seeing that in 2013 they reached the final of the Scottish Youth Cup for the first time since Penicuik won it with me in their squad. We beat Dundee in the final all those years ago. When I reflect, I also realise that playing for Penicuik was a highly formative experience for me. As I've mentioned, I was one of those kids who always took criticism to heart. Penicuik may have been a non-league environment but it was very much a school of hard knocks. Ex-pros would go to play there towards the end of their careers. Being among them toughened me up and made a man of me. Some of those old pros would cut you in two as soon as look at you. I've never been anything like a hatchet man myself and take pride in my disciplinary record. But I like to think I've been a hard competitor who can take the knocks and bounce back.

Perhaps the hardest thing I ever did was also the best and it was well away from any football field. It was that fundamental decision to uproot from a loving family and a settled environment to fly to the other side of the planet. If I hadn't left on that great life adventure I'd never have played against England, Chelsea, Manchester United and Olympiacos. I'd never have lifted that promotion trophy in Cardiff. And I'd never have been writing this book.

So I wouldn't change a thing about my career apart from the futile wish that I'd been blessed with a bit more natural talent. What's more important is that I made the absolute most of the talent I did have. As for those exotic off-field experiences, I'd have to say Australia was the best place to live. That's mainly down to one thing – the weather. I'd go so far as to say that if we had Australia's climate in Britain then we'd be a much happier country and we'd be better at sport. People wouldn't be moping around as much as they seem to do at times. Just watch what happens when the sun comes out. Walk down any street anywhere in the world and people are smiling and look more relaxed. It's as simple as that.

An outdoor life, of the type folk lead in Australia, gives rise to a more outgoing personality. You don't see people with their heads down, looking tense and grumpy. Down Under, they are out having a beer or going to a barbecue. For some, this creates the impression that Aussies are lazy bums. That's far from the truth. They work hard and they play hard. There's a real work ethic in the country. People who go on holiday there invariably want to go back.

That said, I don't see myself living abroad again in the immediate future, and certainly not while my kids are growing up. I don't want to be a disappearing dad, I intend to be there for them. Besides, I have a job here in football and I'm a businessman too. But, further down the line, I wouldn't rule out living and working abroad again. One thing I can say for sure is that it would hold absolutely no fears for me. I've certainly been emboldened by my experiences. Beyond that, travel is the best education you can get. I've heard people say that travel can open a closed mind and I think that's very true. I love going on holiday and going to new places.

Nowhere was more idyllic than Greece. It was like one long holiday living beside the Mediterranean – except that putting your feet up is an alien concept to me. Yes, I enjoyed the beautiful surroundings but I worked hard at my game and made an effort to learn the language. Sometimes it's hard for new players to fit in outside their own countries. That's why I've always believed you have to make an extra effort in that position.

But there can be other reasons why foreign players don't work out in certain surroundings. Sometimes they can have too much of a good time. Take Hong Kong as an example. If you want to really live it up, life for a footballer there can be one long party. I'm talking 24 hours a day every day of the week. There's no such thing as a quiet Sunday in Hong Kong. It's hardly conducive to succeeding as a footballer and that's why most of the foreign players I came across out there never lasted more than a season. They always had spare cash because, apart from earning decent money, your accommodation and travel expenses would be paid by the club. This is where a little Scottishness can come in useful! Haha. Yes, I like a good time (I was acquainted with the 'Dentist's Chair,' as you'll recall) but I was able to stick some money away. This came in very handy when we returned to Scotland. However, the majority of lads came back with nothing at all.

You can perhaps see why it would be easy to describe the game in Hong Kong as the most amateur professional football in the world. I'm not sure but the standard may even have gone further backwards from my time there. That's not to say it wasn't a wonderful experience. The language was something else. I tried to get a handle on some of the spoken word but Cantonese in the written form is a challenge too far. Here, by the way, is how my name looks:

李 布 倫

As I say, I learned to speak a little. It's all about intonation. You can have a word that seems to amount to just one meaning if written down phonetically. But it can have several different meanings depending on how you say it. This would be particularly important if you were taking a taxi ride somewhere. While the younger generation in Hong Kong learn English in school, the older ones – including some taxi drivers – don't have any understanding of our language. That's not a criticism, by the way. No set of people are lazier than the Brits when it comes to language. A lack of any effort at all can go a long way in Hong Kong, and I mean that literally and for the worst. If you make a tiny mistake in pronouncing your destination to a taxi driver then you can end up miles adrift. Be warned.

Partying is one thing. Gambling is another. Race days at Happy Valley are a sight to behold. It's an amazing spectacle. I don't know if this is right or not but people would tell me that there is more money spent in one night at Happy Valley than in the whole racing season in England. Naturally, gambling is big in football too and there would be no end of players getting done for taking back-handers to fix matches. I never came across anything like that myself. Gambling is something I can take or leave. I used to like a wee flutter but I would never go and hammer it. That said, I do love the atmosphere of the casino. There is a buzz about those places. But I can get enough of a tingle by placing just the odd fiver here or there. And anyway, I've never had enough money to chuck at it.

Mind you, football is a gamble however you look at it. So much is down to luck. So much can be decided by being in the right place at the right time. That applies not only on the field but off it as well. It's a game of connections. As in life, who you know can be as important as what you know. But you also have to try to make things happen and I feel a big part of any success I enjoyed was down to that as well. I went out of my way to get it. That is more satisfying than if it just came to me. So … what of the future? Can I have as much success as a coach or manager? Can I have more success even?

Who knows, but I intend to try. Maybe I don't have the advantage of having been a big name player. That can go a long way in the jobs market. But there are a hell of a lot of proven managers out there who have been far more successful in that role than they were as players. I'm hoping that works for me! There are some outstanding examples of this, none better than the case of the 'Special One.'

Jose Mourinho made a total of 94 appearances in Portugal for clubs you've barely heard of, and I've never seen any reference to what position he played. He was a PE teacher who famously became an interpreter for Sir Bobby Robson at Sporting Lisbon and Porto. The rest, as they say, is history. That history includes former Chelsea boss Mourinho becoming the first manager to win the traditional top three championships in European leagues. He was also the first manager to win every domestic trophy in four European leagues (Portugal, England, Italy, Spain). And he was the first to guide four different teams to the semi-finals of the UEFA Champions League, which he won with Porto and Inter. What a man! Some still say you can't hope to understand the game if you haven't played at a certain level. Maybe they are the ones who don't know what they are talking about!

There is no more startling example than Andre Villas-Boas, a young manager I much admire. Incidentally, he was another coaching protégé of Sir Bobby Robson at Porto. Villas-Boas had no experience whatsoever as a professional player. Maybe at the outset that made it harder to gain respect in the dressing room. But if a young boss can overcome that sort of challenge, as Villas-Boas did, then it speaks even more highly of his qualities. With Porto, AVB won four trophies in one season in 2010-11. That year, at the age of 33, he became the youngest manager to win a European competition when he conquered the Europa League.

You don't have to look far to find other examples. In his exceptionally modest playing career, Arsene Wenger turned out for four low-profile outfits. He has managed Arsenal since 1996, which is a huge achievement in itself. Going further back, there was the case of Lawrie McMenemy who had just two years as a player with non-league Gateshead before his career was prematurely ended by injury.

That didn't stop the former guardsman working his way up via Doncaster and Grimsby to have great success with Southampton where he won the FA Cup in 1976. McMenemy lured some top players to the south coast, including Kevin Keegan and the late Alan Ball. That was a sign of the respect he commanded. Lawrie, incidentally, had a formative coaching spell at Sheffield Wednesday in the 1960s.

As is traditional, we save the best until last. Maybe it's not the best example as Sir Alex Ferguson had a decent career as a striker in Scotland, peaking in a couple of years with Rangers. But, by his own admission, he was not blessed with anything like outstanding ability and relied more on determination. Unlike so many of his fellow Scots, he never played south of the border. But that didn't stop him becoming probably the greatest manager England – and the world of football – has ever seen. Oh, and what about his successor at Old Trafford? David Moyes didn't pull up too many trees in a longish career as a centre half. Moyes did win a Championship medal at Celtic as a youngster but tended to fly under the radar after that with spells at

Cambridge United, Bristol City, Shrewsbury, Dunfermline, Hamilton and Preston. We had a near miss in that David joined Dunfermline a year after my first spell at the club ended in 1989.

Far be it from me to draw any sort of comparison between myself and the people I have just mentioned, but perhaps you can see how they are an inspiration to me and so many other young coaches who never scaled the heights as players.

On the flip side, you see some big stars fail to make it as bosses. Their name helps them to land a job in the first place and maybe it can also gain them an extended honeymoon period with the clubs they join. But there is a sense in which their fame, and the money that goes with it, can count against them. If you've only been an average player and have never made the millions some can earn, then you are a hungry manager or coach. But if you are a wealthy bloke at some club in the lower leagues and the crowd start giving you abuse then you can think: 'I'm not having this, I don't need it.' If you're Lee Bullen, you don't walk away. You stick at it.

That is something for boards to think about when they make their choices. I'm not saying there's a throw-in-the-towel mentality with all top players who become managers. Just that it's only human nature to react like that if you are financially secure and don't need any aggravation in your life.

Nobody can say what the future holds but I would love to be in football for the rest of my working life. I'm now 42, having had 23 years as a player. It would be lovely to think I could have a similar length of time coaching or managing. But it's a precarious business, of course. We're in an age when you can get the sack after just three bad results.

It's crazy the way the game has gone and some would say you'd have to be mad to want to be in it. But football is a drug. Once you are hooked you are addicted for life. When you think about it, the lows are as much a part of that as the highs. Without one, you don't get the other.

Maybe it's preaching the obvious but there are only so many teams who can win something or achieve promotion in a given year. The vast majority will be also-rans. But try telling that to the supporters of any team. They will all want or expect to be among the very few winners. That leads to unrealistic expectations at so many clubs and that, in turn, creates the sacking culture.

How can we change that? Well, better communication can go a long way towards levelling things out, in my opinion. Of course, a lot of what goes on at football clubs has to remain in-house and confidential, but supporters are more demanding when it comes to hearing statements of intent. They are hungry for the next morsel of news and desperate to hear that success is around the next corner. In tandem with this, there are season tickets to be sold and commercial deals to be done. Clubs have to be seen to be ambitious and making progress.

There is nothing particularly wrong with any of this. It is only natural, I suppose. But I think it's fair to say that, while fans will always be demanding, they have become a little more savvy when it comes to understanding the financial implications of the game. These dictate that it is very difficult, if not impossible, to succeed on some budgets.

That is not necessarily a barrier to success. It sets a challenge. Coaches can on occasions make the sum of the parts add up to more than their individual value. However, perhaps there needs to be more understanding of this at the outset. I think supporters appreciate it when chairmen are honest and realistic with their expectations. This, in turn, helps create the right environment for the manager.

The more transparent a club can be from the top, the more chance the manager and players have of punching above their weight. Then you can set a viable target for the team rather than a fantasy one that can't be fulfilled. Certainly, the casualty rate is alarmingly high. The many who get sacked can't all be bad managers.

Many have enjoyed previous success which they have the ability, with the right support, to repeat. It's frightening the amount of experienced guys sitting on the sidelines. Then again, I suppose there has to be some change to let the younger ones in. Hopefully the preparation now in place via the Pro Licence will give the next generation a better chance of survival. Don't bet on it, though.

One thing that has changed dramatically – and for the worse – in my time in the game is the standard of Scottish football. As I write, a fairly well established young player in the SPL has just left for a League Two club in England. I refer to Eoin Doyle who was in double figures with his goals for Hibernian last season and yet jumped at a move to Chesterfield. No disrespect to the Spireites here, by the way.

Chaired by ex-Wednesday chief Dave Allen and with my old Owls manager Chris Turner as chief executive, they are ambitious to progress. The Doyle capture demonstrated that. But, until now, anyone would have thought that leaving one of the top four or five clubs in Scotland for one in the English basement would have been a big step down. It's a sign of the times, though.

Celtic and Rangers have also had to lower their sights. Those two are potentially as big as anything in the Premier League, but there is a huge gulf in finances between the two. Players can earn as much, if not more, in the bottom division in England as in the SPL. For a Scotsman like me, this is a sad situation. However, there may be a silver lining to the cloud. Young players in Scotland are getting more opportunities than before and at an earlier age. It is a long road ahead but maybe this will help the Scottish national team in the fullness of time.

As for the clubs up there, well finances dictate. And that's only right, I suppose, because the collapse of a giant like Rangers was an example to all and sundry. In the case of Doyle moving south, Rod Petrie runs a very tight ship at Hibs. Rightly from the business point of view, he ensures that the club continues to be in a strong financial position. He does that even if it means losing a player to League Two in England. Is that right or is that wrong? You tell me. There are no easy answers. Just as long as managers are treated according to those limitations. What is certain in my mind, though, is that something has to be done to freshen up the tired league structure in Scotland. Most of the clubs seem to agree about that but they were at loggerheads on how it should be done at the time I was penning these words.

Just inside my deadline came the outcome of last season's relegation scrap in the Championship which was remarkable even by the standards of an extraordinarily tight division. The relevance is that Sheffield Wednesday were one of seven clubs fighting to avoid the drop on the last day of the season. We never seem to fail the scriptwriters, do we? I celebrated our survival as mightily as any fan – because that is what I have become. You can't develop ties as close as mine have become with this one club not to have a special feeling about them. Ever since that magical day at the Millennium Stadium I have been desperate not to see it go to waste.

There was that escape under Brian Laws in my final season as a player but the momentum was lost in 2010 when the Owls dropped on the last day. Needing to beat rivals Crystal Palace, they were held 2-2 at Hillsborough. As an adopted supporter, that was a sad day for me and I was only too delighted to see the team return a couple of seasons later under Gary Megson and Dave Jones. Once more, it was a question of not letting all the good work go to waste. Being back at the club on the coaching set-up allowed me to see it from the inside. What struck me was that there was never a sense of panic or desperation. I reckon that helped enormously towards the outcome.

Things did look quite worrying at one stage when we lost seven on the bounce. There's often no coming back from that sort of run. But the chairman and manager stayed strong. Form from mid-season onwards was more than steady and the side finished resolutely, losing only two of the last nine. Incredibly, though, even 55 points wasn't enough going into the final day. In the event, a comfortable home win over Middlesbrough in front of over 31,000 eased everyone's nerves. It was Peterborough, who'd beaten us the previous week, who were relegated after sinking to a late defeat at Crystal Palace.

I think in the end it was a reward for staying calm and focused. Managers were dropping like ninepins in the Championship all last season. But there was no chopping and changing at our place in what had to be considered to be a successful adjustment to the higher level. In any ordinary season, 58 points would have been enough for mid-table. A mere 14 points separated 17 clubs between the play-offs and relegation. The margins could not have been finer, suggesting that the degree of improvement required is not that great either. It was a remarkable campaign by any standards.

Once again there was a special atmosphere at Hillsborough to end the season. Wednesday supporters always seem to turn out whether the chips are up or down and I think they have created a real sense of impetus for the challenges to come. Being in the Championship also keeps the bar high for all of us on the academy staff. And it helps the club attract young talent. My greatest sense of satisfaction will come when some of them break into the senior side. I'm confident the club is better equipped than for some time to grow some players of its own.

I'm also continuing to grow into the role. I had to go back to being a youngster when it came to the coaching game but I've probably learned faster than I did as a player. It's an advantage that I have a sense of perspective based around sampling a whole range of cultures on, and off, the field.

And I've learned a helluva lot in my four or five years of further education on the coaching side. If the next 25 years are as eventful and fulfilling as my last 25 in football then I'll be a very happy man. Not that I'm a grumpy old sod anyway. Or at least that's what I like to think. Remember 'The Candy Man?'

And so it comes to saying goodbye – for now. My thanks if you've got this far. And congratulations too. See if you can trade in the book for air miles! It's been good to sit down for just long enough to relive my experiences amid the hustle and bustle of jobs in football and business. Let's see what the future has in store. Bring it on – I'm hungry to do more in the game.

One last request please:

Cover it in chocolate and a miracle or two.

About the Authors

Hailing from Penicuik in Midlothian, Lee Bullen signed for Dunfermline Athletic as a teenager before moving to Meadowbank Thistle and Stenhousemuir. Despite being unable to establish himself in Scottish football, Lee showed the determination to succeed that has been prevalent through his career and signed for Wollongong Wolves in Australia before moving to Hong Kong to play league football for the next four seasons.

Two years playing first division football with Greek side Kalamata preceded a move back to Dunfermline Athletic for four seasons and a Scottish Cup Final appearance in 2004 before being signed by Sheffield Wednesday.

Establishing himself as an integral part of the Hillsborough side, Lee was appointed captain and led the team to victory in the 2005 Play-Off Final, becoming a firm favourite of the Owls' supporters in the process.

Following retirement from playing, Lee moved into football coaching, first as assistant at Falkirk and latterly back at Sheffield Wednesday where he's currently development coach, charged with bringing on the future talent for the club. His Twitter page: @BullenFootball allows fans to keep up to date with progress.

Alan Biggs is a sports journalist, broadcaster and author who has worked on newspapers, radio and television for more than 30 years. He has previously written two books with Vertical Editions: *Confessions of a Football Reporter*, humorous reflections on his colourful career, and was co-author of *Laws of the Jungle* the autobiography of footballer and football manager Brian Laws.

Married with three children, Biggs is a match reporter on BBC television's *Final Score,* having previously worked for Radio 5 Live and also reports games for talkSPORT. He contributes to national newspapers and has a weekly column in the *Sheffield Telegraph.* Alan also lectures on sports journalism at Sheffield Hallam University. His leisure time includes distance running and playing the piano. He also inspires lively football debate on his Twitter page: @AlanBiggs1.